The Munic. ...idence
and the Treasury

Hermann Neumann

Prestel

MUNICH · BERLIN · LONDON · NEW YORK

The Residence Administration
Residenzstrasse 1
80333 Munich
Telephone: (089) 2 90 67-1
Fax: (089) 2 90 67-225
E-mail: ResidenzMuenchen@bsv.bayern.de

Opening hours
April–15 October: 9 am–6 pm
16 October–March: 10 am–4 pm
Open daily

This guide was produced under the auspices of
the Bayerische Schlösserverwaltung.

© contents und design
Prestel Verlag
Munich · Berlin · London · New York, 2001

Front cover: Lion guarding the west façade of
the Residence, *c.* 1594 (see p. 44)
Back cover: The Cabinet of Miniatures

Translated from the German by
Joan Clough-Laub, Munich

Photographic credits: p. 144
Isometric projections: Hermann Neumann

Die Deutsche Bibliothek – CIP Einheitsauf-
nahme data is available

Prestel Verlag
Königinstrasse 9, 80539 Munich,
Tel.: +49 (89) 38 17 09-0
Fax: +49 (89) 38 17 09-35

4 Bloomsbury Place, London WC1A 2QA
Tel.: +44 (020) 7323-5004
Fax: +44 (020) 7636-8004

900 Broadway, Suite 603,
New York, NY 10003
Tel.: +1 (212) 995-2720
Fax: +1 (212) 995-2733
www.prestel.com

Edited by: Christopher Wynne
Design: Albert Teschemacher, Iris von
Hoesslin
Production: Iris von Hoesslin
Printed and bound by:
Passavia Druckservice GmbH

Printed in Germany on acid-free paper

ISBN 3-7913-2170-6 (English edition)
ISBN 3-7913-2207-9 (German edition)

INTRODUCTION

In 1644, Baldassare Pistorini, a musician in the Munich court orchestra, asked Maximilian I, Prince Elector of Bavaria, to be his first son's godfather. In return, the musician presented the Prince Elector with his 'Descriptione Compendiosa', an effusive description of the Munich Residence, the main tracts of which had been finished not long before. Even today this evocative sketch from the 'classical' period of the Bavarian palace is one of the most informative sources on it.

Johann Schmid, the Marquis Ranuccio Sforza Pallavicino and, in 1719, Christoph Kalmbach, steward of the Residence, brought the text up to date. In the two centuries that followed, the Munich Residence of the Bavarian rulers was briefly touched on in travellers' accounts. Writings on the extensive enlargement and renovation work carried out in the neo-classical style were lavishly published. Finally, 1883 saw the publication of Christian Häutle's architectural history of the Residence, which has not been surpassed since then. Publications as comprehensive as those that appeared in the Baroque period have not been attempted since then and those that were made are long since out of print. Not until the Residence Museum, founded in 1920, began to publish 'Official Guides' have reasonably priced and sufficiently comprehensive guidebooks for the vast collections been available. The guidebooks are still published under the auspices of the Bayerische Schlösserverwaltung, the Bavarian Administration of State Castles, Palaces, Gardens and Lakes, who are responsible for the Residence.

The present guidebook has been conceived as a supplement to the others available. First of all, emphasis has been placed on giving an informative account of the history of the building, an undertaking which is not all that simple when one considers the vast size of the Residence and the complexity of its evolution. Historical visual material and model drawings which take the most recent research into account have proved useful.

In view of the bewildering architectural diversity of the Residence and its vast variety of appointments and furnishings, many visitors find selecting essentials a daunting task.

The attempt to organize the material systematically and conveniently linking pictures, text and drawings has been made here in the contemporary spirit. The elaborate interiors, that is, the suites of rooms in period styles in their historical context, are looked at separately from the seven collections, most of which are housed in neutral rooms organized on educational lines. Selected areas of concentration have been intentionally dealt with in depth.

Some sumptuously furnished suites of rooms such as the Prince Electors' and Charlotte Chambers around the Fountain Court have been omitted because the unity of architecture, furnishings and appointments characteristic of the Residence has been impaired or lost over the years. Only a small selection of works from the fields of painting, textiles and sculpture has been handled. The numbering of both rooms and objects used in the 'Official Guide' has been retained. An index of names and a brief bibliography point the way to further study in more detail.

The special collections in the Residence are, in fact, independent museums in their own right, richly endowed with exhibits from their special fields. For this reason we recommend that you plan separate visits to each of them so that you will have enough time to savour the delights of these valuable collections. The present guide focuses on the often turbulent history of the collections as well as elucidating their historic function, some of which, like those of a 'wine cistern' (see p. 119) or a 'pluvial' are represented by terms whose meaning is no longer generally known. This is particularly true of the Reliquary (Reliquienkammer: Room 95). The magnificent artefacts it contains attest to a piety prevailing at that period such that those privileged to visit the Residence in the seventeenth and eighteenth centuries marvelled at it as the greatest treasure.

I should like to express my heartfelt appreciation to all those who have made this book possible. First and foremost, to the Bayerische Verwaltung der staatlichen Schlösser, Gärten und Seen (the Bavarian Administration of State Castles, Palaces, Gardens and Lakes).

If Germany's largest and, despite heavy losses in the second world war, still richest royal city residence thus gains new friends, if old friends are inspired to deepen and broaden their knowledge and if those passing through its rooms should re-member somewhat more of what they have seen, narrowing the selection of rooms and objects presented here, albeit of necessity, will have been well worthwhile.

The present guide is dedicated to the memory of Friedrich Sustris in the 400th year after his death.

'Tellus Bavarica', the symbolic personification of the state of Bavaria, is the work (c. 1590) of Hubert Gerhard. The original surmounts the Diana Temple in the Court Garden and a copy is in the Imperial Hall.

Overleaf, double page: *A bird's-eye view of Munich c. 1700. Copperplate engraving by Michael Wening. A panorama of the Baroque Wittelsbach Residence unfolds before the city's towers; in the foreground is the Court Garden. Dating from c. 1615, it has retained its basic layout to the present day.*

5

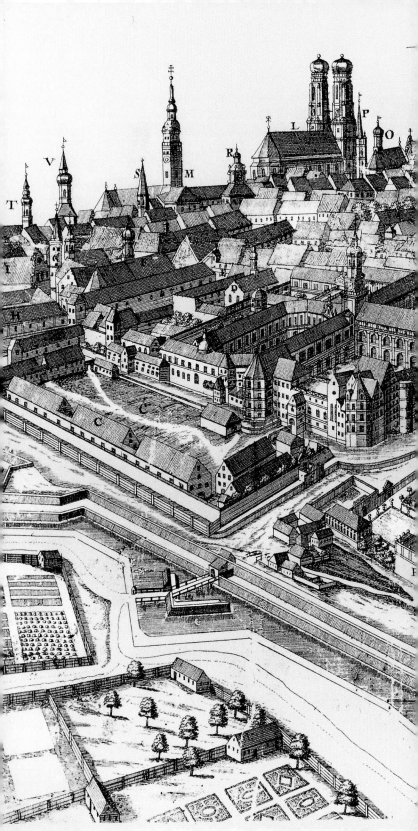

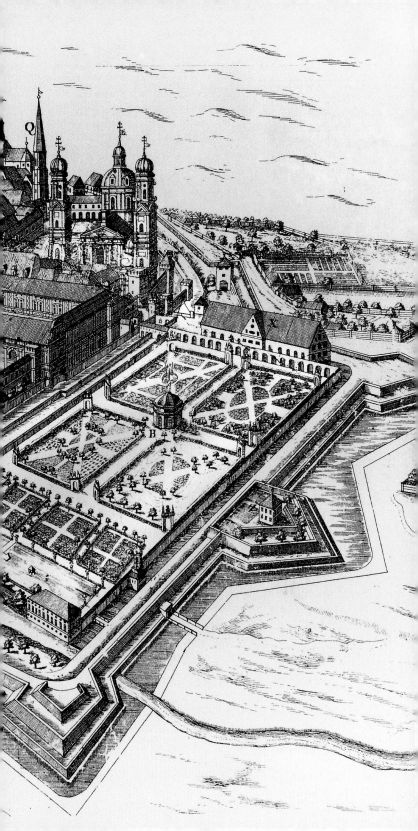

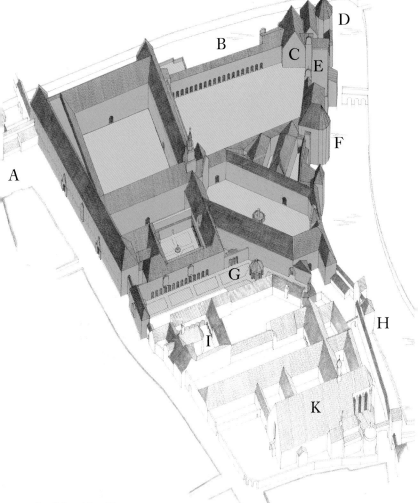

A   Schwabing Gate
B   Hirschgang
C   Hoher Stock
D   St Christopher's Tower
E   St George's Hall in the Neuveste
F   Tower with Round Room
G   The Great Residence Garden with Pegasus Temple
H   City wall with towers, outer bailey and city moat
I   Ridler Monastery
K   Franciscan Church and Monastery

Maximilian's Residence and its surroundings c. 1650. The castle complex is the focal point. Today the square, Max-Joseph-Platz, bounded by the King's Building and the National Theatre, replaces the labyrinthine monastery building to the south.

ARCHITECTURAL HISTORY

**From the 'Neuveste'
to the Antiquarium.
From** *c.* **1385–1598**

Munich owes its elevation to the seat of the Bavarian Court to the Emperor Ludwig the Bavarian (from 1294 as Duke, 1328–47 as Emperor), who enlarged his father's place of residence into the imperial seat. The same holds for the castle, the Alter Hof, whose central court with its tower and two tracts have been preserved in the city centre. Dividing the imperial legacy meant a loss of power to the Emperor's descendants so that his grandsons found it prudent around 1385 to raise defences against a mercantile class that had become proudly assertive. After all, the city, which had grown by leaps and bounds, had denied them freedom of egress.

The Neuveste was fitted into the north-east corner of the outer fortification wall as a redoubt. It overlooked walls fortified with turrets, a moat and, of paramount importance, it was a sally port for escaping unnoticed to the Isar water meadows. When the Residence was rebuilt after World War II, a careful examination was undertaken as to how the complex had been enlarged into a royal seat housing several chapels, a spacious hall, a central clock tower and extensive gardens. The findings were exhaustively recorded (see Bibliography, Otto Meitinger), and are, as such, beyond the scope of this publication.

The architectural history of the palace has a second, more important set of roots, which are closely intertwined with the person of Duke Albrecht V (reigned 1550–79). Through his marriage to a daughter of the Habs-

The Neuveste from the south-west. A bird's-eye view of the building as it was in about 1540, drawn by Wilfried Schaeflein, in charge of the construction of the Residence.

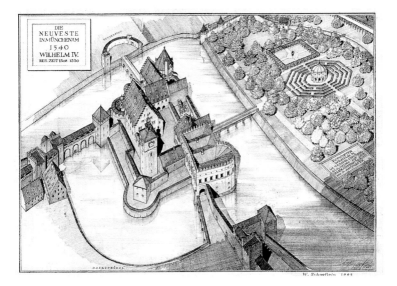

burg Emperor's, this Renaissance prince advanced to a position in which he could fulfil major political ambitions without, however, possessing the means for consolidating the power he coveted. Nonetheless, along with a love for the music of Orlando di Lasso, a passion for collecting – he amassed an important library as well as collections of jewels, coins, antiques and numerous curiosities – he managed to satisfy his curiosity, typical of the time, about all earthly wonders. Phlegmatic by nature, he thus seized a convenient opportunity for distinguishing himself among his more adventurous peers.

However, what he succeeded in collecting on his own could hardly have sufficed to found the later Munich museum collections. Albrecht was fortunate in having as his friend Hans-Jakob Fugger (1515–75), a Humanist and superb organiser. A descendant of the celebrated Augsburg merchant dynasty, he not only made good use of his trade links, he also employed an art agent, Jacobo Strada of Mantua (1515–88) with far-flung connections reaching from the Vatican to the imperial court. Strada was so successful, notably in acquiring Andrea Loredan of Venice's large antiques collection, that a building erected after 1563 near the Alter Hof to house Albrecht's collections soon proved too small. This circumstance paved the way to a new building in which sculpture would be exhibited on the ground floor with the ducal library on the upper floor.

For that purpose the Franciscan monks relinquished a hop garden, situated on the Neuveste tournament grounds, the 'Jägerbühel' (Hunters' Hill). What would be important to its later development was that it was situated at an oblique angle to the castle. Jacobo Strada – by that time architect to the imperial court – did his best to produce plans for an imposing building and also presented ideas for a museum.

Casemates in the south-west corner of the Neuveste, built about 1500. The brick vaulting below the Apothecary Court was exposed and made accessible when the Residence was rebuilt after World War II.

For all his efforts, however, the commission was ultimately granted to the more unassuming Augsburg city architect, Simon Zwitzel. Nevertheless, the Antiquarium Zwitzel built (finished 1571) – a simple, two-storeyed, drawn-out, rectangular structure – is quite grand, especially due to the broad vaulting spanning the entire ground floor. The entrance and stairway are at the south end, where a gallery along the city wall linked all court buildings. The sculpture hall is relatively modestly appointed. Sturdy, whitewashed pilasters support barrel vaulting which is uniform in structure except for bays aligned with the axis of fenestration. A red brick floor stands out against marble pedestals on which statues and busts, skillfully restored by Munich artists, are displayed. All that is known about the appearance of the library is that it was panelled.

Wilhelm V succeeded Albrecht late in 1579 and did so with a flourish. His most impressive contribution to the Residence is the alteration and appointment of the Antiquarium, described in the section on Elaborate Interiors (see p. 34). What is interesting here, however, is his attempt at creating a city palace of Italian appearance separate from the moated castle, which was no longer sufficiently comfortable as a royal dwelling. Political ruin, however, prevented Wilhelm from enjoying the new palace. The projected enlargement of the complex really started in April 1581 with the purchase of a grand house in Schwabinger Gasse, which is now Residenz Strasse. The garden of this house extended from what is now the Chapel Court to the Antiquarium. Not long before, Wilhelm's mother, Anna of Austria, had had two patrician houses in Schwabinger Gasse enlarged and converted into a spacious apartment. On plans by Friedrich Sustris, a landscaped garden boasting open arcades, fountains and pavilions was laid out in the 1580s on the adjoining properties. The Grotto Court and the Grot-

Bust of the Prince Elector Maximilian I from the Stone Rooms. Allessandro Abondio, possibly Balthasar Ableithner, made this sculpture (c. 1640) of the monarch who commissioned the most ambitious building projects at the Residence.

to Hall (see p. 31) have retained their essential character; the 'Great Residence Garden' corresponded to what is now the King's Building Court with an extension to the south-east. The Late Baroque Portrait Gallery (see p. 66) was then an open arcade forming the structural backbone of the complex. A sophisticated iconographic programme of mythological representations created numerous points of reference, which we will deal with in connection with the elaborate interiors.

New building became necessary when the time came for Hereditary Prince Maximilian to be instructed in the arts of governance in about 1591. A showy dwelling was built for him in the area of what is now the Chapel Gate to underscore the suppression of bourgeois housing in favour of the enlargement of the palace. The Chapel Court (see p. 44) with the terrace of houses to the north was then added to

Hans Krumper's 'Patrona Boiariae', the mythical 'Protectress of Bavaria', on the west façade of the palace. Historic photograph.

the court area and, with it, the entire approach to the Neuveste.

Duke Wilhelm's additions did not yet result in one uniform ensemble; too much money and energy had gone into the building of St Michael's, a Jesuit church, and the building Wilhelm had caused to be erected for his retirement. When Maximilian succeeded his father in 1598 on his abdication, he found a well-prepared site to accommodate the much more extensive building he was planning.

Duke Maximilian's 'Marvel of a Building'. From 1598–1651

Maximilian I (1573–1651), who acquired the hereditary electoral title for his line in 1623, was one of the most impressive figures in Bavarian history. Reforming the administration of his dukedom, he was also a financial ge-

nius who consolidated political conditions under his rule, which saw him enhance his power in the service of the emperor during the Thirty Years' War despite the dramatic decimation of more than half the Bavarian population. Harsh and strictly based on religion, Maximilian's regime was suited to the constraints of a turbulent age. Pursuing an interest in art as ambitiously as his predecessors yet far more systematically, he concentrated on enlarging and renovating the Residence. During the first two decades of the seventeenth century, he achieved this goal.

Maximilian's first architectural project on a large scale, finishing the Antiquarium, was achieved by 1600 with the aid of Bavarian craftsmen and artisans. The floor of the hall was lowered to monumental effect. The marble stucco end walls, the stairs and the table dais were built and the ceiling paintings took on their final form.

What was already there was then standardized in one great effort: the Hereditary Prince's House in Schwabinger Gasse was renovated and extended to the south; new silver vaults were built (ecclesiastical vestments are now exhibited there, see p. 106) and suitable apartments for Duchess Elisabeth of Lorraine were fitted out on the main floor. In about 1640 renovation work was again undertaken here to refurbish the apartments for Maximilian's second wife, Maria Anna of Austria. Across a small court, which led into the midst of the complex of houses, Duchess Anna's dower house was demolished and replaced by a gallery which closed off the Great Residence Garden to the west. Beyond the stair to the Silver Vaults the new Court Chapel (see p. 45) was added, which had probably been preceded on the site by a more modest structure. A slightly receding chancel was added to it in 1630. Close by, a superb late Renaissance interior was consecrated in the upper storey in 1607: the ducal private oratory, called Reiche Kapelle (Rich Chapel, see p. 49).

Begun under Duke Wilhelm, renovation work on the Grotto Court continued: the wall separating it from the Chapel Court was raised by a full storey to incorporate a narrow linking passage. A roof garden was laid out on the other side above the earlier suite of rooms. At the back a gallery was built to house the duke's most precious art treasures. His private apartments and audience chambers were built to the east above the Grotto Hall. The library was removed from above the Antiquarium shortly before 1600 and replaced by apartments for guests. Representative ceremonial assembly chambers

were necessary for what was now the core area of the new palace. The Black Hall with its perspective painting assumed this function in the southern part of the complex and a spacious stair was built leading up to it. The more imposing Broad Stair was built at the other end of the Antiquarium wing; it led up to the large reception room, which opens out of an earlier hall with a raised ceiling north of the Chapel Court. Its appointments included a cycle of tapestries with mythological motifs which have given it the name Herkulessaal, the Hall of Hercules. The new dining room (now the

Orlando di Lasso in concert in St George's Hall in the Neuveste. Miniature by Hans Mielich for an illuminated manuscript of works by the famous Munich Court musician, c. 1560. This first Banqueting Hall was in the east wing of the moated Neuveste.

Hans Krumper's design for the stucco decoration of the Stone Rooms. Collection of Graphic Art of the Munich City Museum.

Knights of St George Hall) was the link between it and the ducal apartments. A gallery linking the new complex with the Neuveste surrounded the tournament square at the Jägerbühel to form an elongated octagon which has been preserved as the Brunnenhof (Fountain Court, see p. 44).

Following a phase of interior renovation (now for the most part lost), the second stage of building was embarked on towards 1612 after the acquisition of quite extensive property. The tracts planned for the north were aligned to give on to the new Court Garden, which was far larger than the earlier open ground. After its incorporation within the city fortification, the old north wall was demolished to make room for a spacious hall. The Imperial Stair now led up to the Imperial Hall (see p. 52). More generous than the old Antiquarium, it glittered sumptuously with magnificent gilding. The combination of staircase and hall inaugurated the practice of staging the process of ascending and descending between levels which would culminate in the architecture of Würzburg and Pommersfelden Palaces. The Vier-Schimmel-Saal (The Hall of the Four Greys) abutting on the west is reached by the Hans Steininger Stair where the portrait of Hans Steininger, the mayor of Braunau, can be seen, who, the story goes, fell to his death by tripping over his long beard. Elegant guest apartments uniting various earlier architectural features link the new Court Garden tract with the (old) Hercules Hall. Their ceiling paintings and important tapestries make the Trier Rooms (see p. 58) and the Stone Rooms to the west (see p. 54) two of the most exquisite suites in the Residence.

The vast square formed by the Kaiserhof (Imperial Hall, see p. 44) boasts nine rows of double windows along each façade. With two full floors and mezzanines, it towers over the rest of the complex, monumentally incorporating, on the city side, all that had been built before it. Thus the showy street façade of the Residence was created as can be seen today with its 33 axes (see p. 43), two marble portals and the centrally positioned statue of the 'Patrona Boiariae'.

A final effort at incorporating the Neuveste made it necessary to demolish the keep and old living quarters. The rubble was used to fill the moat to the south-west. The new façade with the centrally positioned St George's Hall closes the Apothecary Court to the east. Of the linking passages the Charlotte Corridor was preserved. With its central clock tower finished, the complex became the most magnificent palace north of the Alps before the Thirty Years' War. Its fame as a 'marvel of a building' rested primarily on the superb appointment and furnishing of the rooms as well as an iconographic programme consistently rich in associations. What has remained is described in the section covering the elaborate interiors. This ingeniously organised complex has occasioned a great deal of speculation and has been compared to a city within a city. Heinrich Schön the Elder, who functioned as the Chief Administrator of the Court Architectural Office, and Hans Krumper, sculptor and inventive designer, can only be credited individually with some of this stupendous achievement. A courtier, when asked by King Gustavus Adolphus of Sweden as to who had designed the Residence which the monarch so admired, was probably right in answering that the Prince Elector himself had been its architect.

Conversion into an Imperial Seat. From 1651–1777

The Prince Elector Ferdinand-Maria (1636–79), the peace-loving successor to Maximilian I, bowed in matters of taste to his energetic wife, Henriette-Adelaide of Savoy. Her lasting contribution to Munich architecture was the Theatine Court Church, commissioned in gratitude for the birth of an hereditary prince. It brought the weighty grandeur of Northern Italian Baroque to Bavaria. Not until the death of her mother-in-law in 1665 was the Electress able to redesign her personal apartments in the new style. Early descriptions of the Residence dwell fondly on the enigmatic universe of mythological motifs adorning these eleven rooms, cabinets and galleries. Heavily gilded carving dominated the bedchamber. After World War II all that was left of it were some doors and paintings. A later description of the adjoining Herzkabinett (Heart Cabinet, see p. 64), which was the only one of the rooms to have survived relatively intact, gives some idea of its splendour. The building was only slightly modified externally when the Goldener Saal (Golden Hall, see p. 63) was built south of the long city façade. Its ceiling painting can still be seen. Major parts of the suite were destroyed in the great fire of 1674, which devastated the main floor of the tract along Residenz Strasse. The Prince Elector and his wife, both of whom died young, had to leave its reconstruction to their heir, Maximilian Emmanuel.

The Golden Hall designed for Henriette-Adelaide, Electress of Bavaria. Historic photograph. Only the ceiling paintings of the audience chamber (1667) are still in place.

The 'Blue Elector' (1662–1726), a bold soldier, made his name as a field commander in the war against the invading Ottoman forces. He also prudently represented Habsburg interests as 'Stadholder' in what is now Belgium. The War of the Spanish Succession, however, forced him into exile in France. From there he returned in 1715 full of aesthetic inspiration for refurbishing the Residence which would provide it with its most magnificent rooms. His first undertaking was to rebuild the royal private apartments and audience chambers. The young Elector charged the architect Enrico Zuccalli, who had worked for his parents, with designing them in 1680. An annexe was built to the suite of antechambers and audience chambers above the Grotto Hall in the south-east towards the Antiquarium tract. These are known as the Alexander Rooms. Their ceiling paintings were representations of the Hellenistic conqueror king with whom Max Emmanuel identified himself. The gallery in the Grotto Court south wing was extended to include four drawing and sitting rooms, known as Summer Rooms, and a terrace was created at roof level. A painting by Johann Anton Gumpp (Mars with 'Consilium' and 'Inventio', from what would ultimately become the Hall of the Knights of St George), now in Nymphenburg, and the western-most Summer Room with stucco decoration have survived. A chapel to St Cecilia was reconstructed by 1966 on a simplified plan and everything else was sacrificed to rebuilding. Nonetheless, quite a bit of furniture and the Stone Rooms, which were restored in about 1700, convey a good idea of what the High Baroque Residence looked like. It well bears comparison with Max Emmanuel's prime aesthetic achievement, the New Palace at Schleissheim, which was designed by the court architect Joseph Effner (1687–1745).

In the year of his death, the Prince Elector commissioned Effner to renovate his private apartments a second time. On this occasion the wall dividing the Summer Rooms from the adjoining gallery was demolished to create a suite of south-facing rooms. Indispensable ancillary rooms and a council room or privy chamber give onto the Grotto Court. Up until World War II the carved panelling above the Grotto Hall was still visible. The audience chambers, which have been reconstructed to the same proportions, are, therefore, still called the Effner Rooms.

A second fire broke out in the Residence in 1729, destroying the rooms in the south wing and a number of important works of art. Karl Albrecht (1697–1745), the reigning Prince Elector, immediately commissioned a new architect with the rebuilding. François Cuvilliés (1695–1768), a Walloon, had been brought to Munich by Max Emmanuel on his return from exile and educated as an architect at the Prince Elector's expense at the Académie Royale. Cuvilliés' treatment of the French Regency, incorporating basic elements of the traditional Munich court style, laid the groundwork for the development of Bavarian Rococo, the region's most valuable contribution to art. A new gallery wing with a magnificent staircase bisecting the Great Residence garden is, with the removal of the roof terrace, the salient feature of the renovation finished in 1737. At the same time, the long façades on the Grotto Court and the exterior of its west wing were renovated in an enlightened manner, borrowing from the late Baroque period. More importantly, the interior of the south tract, named after the Portrait Gallery (see p. 66) was refurbished. Its Rich Rooms (see p. 69) and the new Green Gallery (see p. 73) are described in detail in the section on the elaborate interiors.

Unfortunately, the stairwell in the enclosed courtyard could not accommodate the ceremonial approach of state carriages. Therefore, it was soon converted into a dining room and, by the nineteenth century, had disappeared altogether. Karl Albrecht's private living quarters, the Yellow Apartment (in which eighteenth-century porcelain is now displayed: see p. 128), was sacrificed to the same insensitivity. It would seem that all that is left of it is possibly one double door which is now in the Metropolitan Museum in New York.

Karl Albrecht's era ended in disaster. His election as emperor of the Holy Roman Empire, defeating his powerful Habsburg relatives, seemed at first to have made a centuries-old Wittelsbach dream come true. Instead it plunged Bavaria into war and an economic downturn. For all that, the Emperor Charles VII, who had lost most of his land, was left to die in peace in his own Rich Rooms in 1745.

The new Prince Elector, Max III Joseph (1727–77) had to make considerable economies. Showing filial piety, he had the rooms above the Antiquarium, the Electoral Rooms, renovated for himself and his wife, Maria Anna of Saxony, in order to leave his parents' apartments untouched. Rococo rooms suitable for everyday living dominated in an exactly corresponding but reversed arrangement of antechamber, audience chamber, bedroom and adjacent cabinets. Now that the rooms have been reconstructed the priceless original furniture has come into its own as the dominant feature of the rooms on the Fountain Court side. The rooms at the back have been redecorated to house the East Asian Collection (see p. 122).

In 1750 fire broke out once again, the last time but one to date. It started in the Neuveste, in St George's Hall, used as a theatre at that time, when materials to create special effects were improperly handled. The fire destroyed almost the entire original part of the fortress complex. Patched up in a makeshift manner, the old redoubt was subsequently relegated to the status of

Portrait of the Prince Elector Karl Albrecht, from the Residence Portrait Gallery. Briefly Emperor of the Holy Roman Empire, he is better remembered for his patronage of the architect François Cuvilliés.

an outbuilding. More importantly, this meant that a new court theatre had to be built, perhaps as an act of defiance, or perhaps to make an impression on wavering allies in Vienna and Versailles. That it failed to do so did not prevent François Cuvilliés from assembling the leading Bavarian court artists to create a perfect gem of mature Rococo. This distinguished group of artisans included Joachim Dietrich, the ornament carver, cabinet-makers in Adam Pichler's circle, Johann Baptist Zimmermann the fresco painter and, most notably, the sculptor Johann Baptist Straub. To ensure safety in case of fire, the theatre was built into the far south-eastern corner of the complex, a location which did not leave enough room for a suitably elegant façade. However, the exquisite interior, is all the more sumptuous for its plain packaging, sparkling in white, red and gold with festive yet bucolic gaiety.

About ten years later the most important architect to have worked on

The (old) ResidenceTheatre, a Rococo masterpiece by Cuvilliés, was the Prince Elector Max III Joseph's most important contribution to the Residence.

the Residence embarked on a final undertaking.

Plans for a monumental new building along the eastern tract were drawn up, the first building in 150 years on a scale to match the tracts built for Maximilian I. A model is exhibited in the Knights of St George Hall (Room 54) in the Residence Museum and some drawings have been preserved. It centres around the new Court Chapel with compact wings radiating out and enclosing a level ceremonial court. The back would have incorporated the Apothecary Court in a setting commensurate with the eighteenth-century love of clarity. The north façade of the complex would finally have attained a length of some four hundred metres, rivalling even Versailles. Even had the state coffers been full instead of depleted to relieve famine, the last descendant of the Bavarian branch of the Wittelsbachs, an enlightened lover of the arts, would not have been able to pull off such a tour de force.

The Palace of the Bavarian Kings. From 1799–1944

Max IV Joseph (1756–1825), who was the next Prince Elector in line, proclaimed Bavaria an independent kingdom on New Year's day 1806. Descended from a Palatinate collateral line of the Wittelsbachs and a soldier at heart, Max IV Joseph and his large family brought life into what would otherwise have been a gloomy palace. Surprised in 1799 to find the skein of tangled family lines in his hand, he was fortunate in having in Maximilian, Count Montgelas, an experienced statesman as his privy councillor. A loyal ally of Napoleon's, Maximilian Joseph succeeded in enlarging his kingdom until it reached the size of the present Free State of Bavaria (including the Rhenish Palatinate).

Queen Karoline of Baden ensured that the Bavarian court maintained a fittingly elegant lifestyle. Plans for extensive building and renovation work were part of it; realisation of them was ultimately restricted to the north tract of the Imperial Court. At first, Charles-Pierre Puille, an experienced interior decorator who had worked for Maximilian, was in charge of appointing this suite, known as the Court Garden Rooms. He was replaced from 1805 by Andreas Gärtner (1744–1826), who had trained in France. Heedless of tradition, the present occupiers abandoned the two Late Renaissance ceremonial halls to make room for an antechamber, a spacious salon, an audience chamber, bedrooms and assorted cabinets for the Queen. King Maximilian and their daughters moved into the mezzanine above. The north façade of the palace was refurbished so that it was now articulated in the stringent neo-classical style. After renovation work carried out under King Ludwig II and the destruction during World War II, the fine interiors were abandoned. Some of the salvaged furnishings and appointments from it are now exhibited with other early nineteenth-century furniture in the Charlotte Chambers to the east of the Fountain Court.

The work of government was carried out between 1810 and 1918 in the southern section of the tract facing Residenz Strasse. Here Gärtner created the Council State Chambers, austere halls with silk-covered walls in which the Bavarian throne was pulled up cosily to the Council table. Unfortunately, the furnishings could not be returned to their original, historic setting as the silver collection of the Residence (see p. 117) has been displayed here since 1974.

Two other interiors designed by Andreas Gärtner are noteworthy. First, in the north-east corner formed by the Imperial Court tracts, the White Hall (c. 1810) is a cool echo of the Trier Rooms in marble stucco which is bare today and, reduced in size, serves as a cloakroom. At about the same time the Old Hercules Hall was remodelled and assumed the function of ceremonial hall. The white room, its walls articulated by pilasters and now known as the Max Joseph Saal, is popular as a venue for concerts (see photo p. 29). After World War II, the two galleries along the narrow sides had to be removed when the room was restored because of a new staircase. This change and earlier segregation from the Residence Museum have dissociated the room from its historic and architectural context.

The most important contribution made by King Maximilian I to the Resi-

Cuvilliés' last project, enlarging the palace complex to replace the Neuveste, burnt to the ground in 1750, was, unfortunately, not carried out. The model is in the Knights of St George Hall.

The Residence in about 1854, viewed from the north. A section of the city model made by Johann-Baptist and Franz Seitz, in the Bayerisches Nationalmuseum. Leo von Klenze's remodelling of the Residence into a royal palace had been completed.

dence complex can only be briefly touched on here. After the Franciscan monastery was disbanded, the way was clear for some major building projects south of the Residence. From 1811 Carl von Fischer (1782–1820) worked on the National Theatre next to Cuvilliés' court theatre. The largest of its day, no sooner had Fischer's masterpiece been finished than it burnt to the ground and the architect died soon afterwards. Quickly rebuilt, the National Theatre gave the Palace and its surroundings a different character altogether, furnishing the main axis of what would become Max-Joseph-Platz. Monumental improvements to the surroundings of the square were expressly reserved for Maximilian's successor, King Ludwig I (1786–1868, reigned 1825–48). From 1823 Ludwig had been working on designs for new royal apartments with his architect, Leo von Klenze (1784–1864).

Although the king and the master architect were as different characters as two people could be, the tensions generated between them proved productive. Ludwig, excitable and given to bursts of enthusiasm, wanted to lead his country to new cultural heights. An ambitious architect, Klenze was constrained to mould the building projects laid before him into something suiting his own fastidious ideas of form. Greco-Roman antiquity as echoed in the Italian Renaissance was the touchstone against which this unlikely collaboration succeeded. Although Klenze detested eighteenth-century architecture, Ludwig protected it from demolition. Cuvilliés' Green Gallery was among the important works he saved.

From 1826 building work was carried out within sixteen years on a scale as grand and as aesthetically consistent in its concept as the achievements of Ludwig's great role model, the Prince Elector Maximilian. This spate of building was inaugurated with All Saints' Court Church, Klenze's most important ecclesiastical building, consecrated on 1 November 1837 (see p. 83). Abutting on the last open side of the Fountain Court, it counterbalanced the new Court Riding School on Marstallplatz, which the architect had finished during the lifetime of King Maximilian I. After much discussion on style (the king was toying with a replica of the Norman Capella Palatina in Palermo) and where the main entrance should be, Munich was presented with its template of Historicism, which, resplendent in native Bavarian green sandstone, melted the domed spaces of San Marco in Venice with the façade of Cremona Cathedral. The Heinrich Hess frescoes that adorned it were on a gold ground. Didactically expansive on the theme of the Passion and the Redemption of Man, they spearheaded the king's campaign for ecclesiastical renewal. Even today, stripped of all decoration, the splendidly proportioned interior achieves an effect of stunning monumentality.

The "Königsbau" (King's Building, see p. 81) with private apartments and audience chambers of the royal household, also begun in 1826, had to be fitted into the structures already extant. Since the gallery along Residenz Strasse and the south perpendicular wing of the Green Gallery were in the way, they were demolished. Utilization of space proceeded on the model of the Crown Prince's apartments in the Electoral Rooms, which meant on Baroque lines. Here too the stairs are positioned at the ends of suites and the royal apartments were adjacent and intimate in design. Queen Therese's new apartments received their own façade with seven windows giving on to Residenz Strasse. Her private rooms were reached via the Queen Mother's Stair, probably thus named because the

An intimate glimpse into the private apartments prepared for King Maximilian I soon after 1800 in the Court Garden tract. Watercolour by Ernst Bandel (c. 1820) from the 'Wittelsbach Album', Wittelsbacher Ausgleichsfonds.

mother of King Ludwig II lived in that part of the complex until 1889. The external appearance of the new wing reveals unmistakable similarities with Florentine models yet, on closer scrutiny, these are less significant than they may at first seem.

The approach to the king's apartments started at the southern end of the Fountain Court. The first monumental room on the way was the early seventeenth-century Black Hall, from which the Yellow Stair with its dramat-

King Ludwig I in full regalia. Joseph Stieler painted this state portrait from the First Battle Hall in 1826.

ically pitched dome led to a portal framed by guardian spirits and Ludwig's motto 'Gerecht und Beharrlich' (Just and Persistent). Unfortunately, reconstruction of this stairwell after World War II left it bereft of its grandeur. The central stair at the back of the King's Building leading to the ancillary rooms and apartments was, on the other hand, little altered. Today it takes visitors up to the Bavarian

Academy of the Fine Arts, housed on the second floor. Even before he ascended the throne, Crown Prince Ludwig was determined that his new palace would boast monumental fresco cycles on the scale of those he had admired in Rome and Mantua. What remained of these paintings, especially in the Nibelung Halls (see p. 83), would come to be regarded as a legacy of neo-classical interior decoration.

That the north side of the palace still left much to be desired becomes apparent when one looks at Domenico Quaglio's painting of Court Garden Strasse. From 1835 the appearance of this tract was improved by the addition of the Festsaalbau (Banqueting Hall Building, see p. 81). This was yet another project of Leo von Klenze's which enhanced the growing pride Bavarians and their rulers took in their young kingdom since, until it was undertaken, there had been no suitable setting for grand ceremonial occasions. The Throne Room was of paramount importance in this connection. The only suitable place for it was the central tract of the new wing. All that has re-

Leo von Klenze, photograph, 1856. Franz Hanfstaengl Estate, Munich City Museum.

Domenico Quaglio painted this romantic view of the north elevation of the Residenz, seen from the east, in about 1828 before its appearance was radically changed by Klenze's Banqueting Hall Building. Neue Pinakothek, Munich.

mained of its appointments, apart from the throne, is a series of more than life-size statues of the Wittelsbach rulers, designed by Ludwig Schwanthaler. Today they stand in the lobby of the concert hall which was built on the site and completed in 1953. The rooms beyond the Throne Room were dedicated to such romantically tinged colossi of imperial history as Charlemagne, Frederick Barbarossa and Rudolf of Habsburg. On the ground floor there was even enough space for cycles of paintings on the Odyssey, which the king wanted as a counterpoint to the Nibelung theme. These rooms were never finished and were destroyed. A second focal point of the Banqueting Hall Building was for social occasions, a Ball Room with adjacent cabinets displaying the King's Gallery of Beauties (now exhibited in Nymphenburg). The east wing was finished off with the Battle Hall; its history paintings dealing with the Napoleonic Wars are now in the King's Building.

The main stairwell was positioned in the south-east corner of the new tracts, an inconvenient way of ensuring that the impressive grand halls were not interrupted. This may be one of the reasons why, after the war, the Banqueting Hall Building was deemed unsuitable for modern purposes and gutted before being entirely redecorated.

The only substantial contribution made by King Maximilian II (reigned 1848–1864) to the Residence was seemingly not appreciated; his Conservatory linking the royal apartments with the two court theatres was demolished in the 1920s. The achievements of his son, the unfortunate 'fairy-tale monarch', suffered a similar fate. It is known that King Ludwig II found no pleasure in politics and modern urban life and, therefore, detested the entire Residence complex and what it stood for. Nonetheless, on ascending the throne in 1864, he made himself comfortable in the remote upper floor of the Theatine tract near Odeonsplatz. An audience chamber, a dining room, bedroom and study were designed and appointed for his use, soon to be followed by a conservatory with a huge steel skeleton. Since it even contained a large pond, construction of the conservatory made extensive supporting structures necessary, considerably diminishing the elegance of the garden façade. Eduard Riedel's Historicism rooms and their appointments would, of course, today be among the most popular tourist attractions in the Residence. They were not, however, reconstructed after 1945. The Hanging Gardens had disappeared shortly after 1886, the year Ludwig II died, although the massive substructure of the Conservatory was not removed until after World War II. The restoration measures commissioned by the king to be carried out in the late Baroque sections of the complex which Ludwig liked are worthy of mention.

The Bavarian monarchy never recovered from the decline of court life which set in under Ludwig II. He was succeeded by Luitpold, the Prince Regent, since Otto, the next Wittelsbach in succession, was mentally unstable. Still reigning in his eighties and nineties Luitpold embodied fin de siècle Munich. In 1897 he commissioned Julius Hofmann with building a new Treasury and restoring the façades with due deference to period style.

The Bavarian Free State cleverly came to terms with the House of Wittelsbach, which was deposed in 1918. By 19 May 1920 the Residence Museum was open to the public, albeit at first only the main floor without the Banqueting Hall Building. Modest restoration work and changes needed for the museum were carried out until there were 157 display rooms in all, comprising two different sections. Finished in 1937, they formed the world's largest museum of furnished and ap-

The colonnaded Ball Room in the Residence Banqueting Hall Building. The photograph was taken directly before the building was destroyed in 1944. This space is now one of the concert hall lobbies.

Working drawings of the great Entrance Hall on the ground floor of the King's Building, c. 1830, Archives of the Bavarian Castles Administration. Very few plans which were used as much as these have been preserved, unlike plans for show.

pointed historic rooms. When the museum was closed (and probably often enough during opening hours), the old seat of the Bavarian rulers became a Sleeping Beauty left untouched even by the National Socialists in their abortive efforts to transform Munich.

World War II soon prevented any productive development of this unique cultural institution. The central air-raid warning shelter for Munich was established in the cellar of the Banqueting Hall Building, which suffered its first direct hit in 1943. The Bavarian Administration of State Castles, Gardens and Lakes then gave top priority to recording the buildings and ultimately to ensuring that such appointments and furnishings as could be moved were stored for safe keeping. All this work was in progress when, on 25 April 1944, the Residence was gutted by fire during one of the worst bombing raids on Munich.

**A Phoenix Rising from the Ashes:
A Centre of Culture.
From 1945 to the Present**

Shortly after the Residence had been devastated by fire, an organisation was founded which was to devote its efforts solely to reconstructing the wrecked palace complex. Bombing raids continued, accompanied by rain and frost which wrought their worst on what

had survived until then, especially stucco work and frescoes. Not until the war ended in May 1945 could the situation be accurately assessed. Nearly all roofs had been destroyed, most of the woodwork burnt, many of the vaulted ceilings had collapsed, the Residenz Strasse façade lay partly in ruins, the Grotto Hall and the two theatres had been reduced to rubble. The American military command helped as much as time and expertise permitted.

Hopeful signs were now essential. A group of Munich residents committed to their city's cultural achievements formed an organisation known as 'Friends of the Residence' to hold concerts in the Grotto Court, which had been cleared of rubble. The Brunnenhof Theatre, a repaired furniture magazine, temporarily housed the Bavarian State Theatre. The director Paul Verhoeven brought pieces which had not been performed for years to exciting fruition on a tiny stage. Next door, a team of young architects was hard at work. The beginnings looked inauspicious yet the conviction grew that, despite material shortages and the priority accorded to housing, commitment to rebuilding the royal palace was not as touchingly quixotic as it had seemed.

Rudolf Esterer (1879–1965), President of the Administration of Castles, threw himself wholeheartedly into the rescue mission. One of the last Court Architects, he considered himself heir

A view over what was left of the roofs of the Residence shortly after the bombing raid in April 1944. In the foreground are the Rich Rooms and behind them the Imperial Court tracts, the Field Marshal's Hall and the Theatine Church.

to the tradition of Cuvilliés and Klenze. His task was to find an aesthetically satisfactory compromise between a new building and the preservation of the old, based on the superlative tradition of Bavarian craftsmanship.

By 1950 things were really looking up for the Residence. The Antiquarium had a new roof and its collapsed vaulting had been reconstructed. Above the Chapel Gate the abbreviated angle of a building indicated the course to be taken in the reconstruction of the Imperial Court and Residenz Strasse. Cuvilliés Court Theatre on Max-Joseph-Platz was converted into a modern state theatre. It was left to the 'German Economic Miracle', however, to bring on a spate of building activity which triumphed over the devastation wrought by war. The new concert hall in the Banqueting Hall Building led the way. Here Rudolf Esterer rebuilt the old Throne Room, incorporating the Trier Tract to provide space for ancillary rooms. Although he sacrificed the neo-classical interior and even the old layout to the need for cloakrooms and a new stairway, he did succeed in linking numerous motifs from the old period style. The façades, by contrast, were – in the same way as virtually the entire palace – restored as far as possible to their historical appearance.

The inauguration in 1953 of the concert hall, which was called the (new) Hercules Hall (named after the decorative cycle of tapestries) marked the turning-point in the most recent architectural history of the Residence. The planners succeeded triumphantly in reviving a complex built for a defunct purpose by informing it in its new guise with the same civilised spirit, subtly attuned to changes in a sophisticated society, which had been the paramount characteristic in its heyday. Distinguished organisations soon moved in: in 1959 the Bavarian Academy of Sciences and Humanities took over the north-east of the Banqueting Hall Building. Generous office space has been provided on the top floor for the Max-Planck Society, the powerhouse of creative German interdisciplinary research in science and the hu-

Reconstruction work beginning on the collapsed Antiquarium; the new roof truss of prefabricated concrete elements is being put into position. The photo was probably taken in 1946.

manities. The Bavarian Academy of the Fine Arts is magnificently accommodated on the third floor of the King's Building. To round off its triumphant cultural rebirth, the Residence also houses the fine Bavarian state numismatic and Egyptian art collections. What took longest to return home, however, was the very soul of the Residence as the seat of the Bavarian court, the works of art and regal appointments which had been saved from its ashes. Since 1958 was the eight-hundredth anniversary of the founding of Munich, energy and funds were forthcoming. The façades and roofs were all restored in time for the celebrations. The Residence Museum reopened to mark the occasion with an exhibition on 'European Rococo' and the exquisite Cuvilliés Theatre was once again the enchanting setting for performances of Mozart operas.

Chamber music in Max Joseph Hall. The Banqueting Hall of the Dukes of Bavaria, it was known as the Hercules Hall until the new hall was inaugurated under that name in 1953.

The restorers fought to preserve the major achievements of the three major periods that moulded the Residence in their original state: the late Renaissance is represented by the Antiquarium, the Grotto Court and the Court Chapel; late Baroque by the Portrait Gallery and the Porcelain Cabinet and neo-classicism by the masterly fresco paintings in the Nibelung Halls. Restoring the airy filigree of ceiling stucco adorning the Cabinet of Mirrors also laid the groundwork for gradually reconstructing what is probably the most important suite of rooms in the Residence, the Rich Rooms (Reiche Zimmer). The collections were also returned to where they belonged. In addition, solid examples of conservative interior decoration as in the Banqueting Hall building were created in the New Treasury of the King's Building (see p. 94) and the eighteenth-century porcelain rooms (see p. 128). Reconstructing and adding to the Museum proceeded apace in four main stages: by 1966 the rooms around the Fountain Court had been restored; by 1974 the two Imperial Court wings with their guest apartments and the remaining collections; 1980 saw the completion of work on the Royal Apartments and, by 1985 the ceremonial rooms built for the Prince Elector Maximilian I around the Imperial Hall were open to the public again.

This last project was dear to the hearts of art historians who had worked for the old Residence Museum and had never ceased to regret King Maximilian's arbitrary cut into the Imperial Court rooms. Rudolf Esterer's plan for reconstruction, drawn up the 1940s, had not been able to rely on sufficient historical data to be acceptable by modern preservation standards. Viewed from the perspective of the reconstruction as a whole, it represents a bold remodelling – a well-executed addition which has blended in harmoniously. The same holds for the Cuvilliés Theatre; it was, in fact Esterer's idea. It has given the fronts of the boxes which were saved from the ruins of the Court theatre an entirely appropriate new home on the neo-classical Apothecary Tract.

ELABORATE INTERIORS

Late Renaissance Rooms
(1570–97)

THE GARDENS OF WILHELM V,
DUKE OF BAVARIA

Friedrich Sustris and the Grotto Hall

While still Hereditary Prince, Wilhelm V, Duke of Bavaria, developed a sophisticated lifestyle. Coming to power in 1579 he did not wish to be immured in the gloomy Munich palace. Having already modernized Burg Trausnitz in Landshut, he set about recreating his new surroundings in the Italian manner. Wilhelm's adviser in matters of art, Friedrich Sustris (*c.* 1540–1600), was ideally suited to carrying out his patron's plans. The son of an Amsterdam painter thought to have been born in Italy, Sustris was trained in Florence under Vasari. Having made his name in the Fuggers' circle, Sustris was extraordinarily gifted as a designer and architect. Under his supervision, a group of artists shaped Munich court art for the rest of the century. Unfortunately, little is known about Sustris, a contemporary of Tintoretto and El Greco. Very little of his work has come down to us yet the parts of the Residence discussed here must surely be among his most important achievements.

The Grotto Court (Grottenhof: Room 6), at the very heart of the Residence, is the most sumptuously decorated of the courtyards. For a long time it was closely associated with the living quarters of the Dukes of Bavaria. The

Mercury, messenger of the gods, leaps out of the magnificent grotto pier after which court and hall are named. The gilt bronze statue is attributed to Hubert Gerhard.

various rebuilding schemes during the palace's history scarcely touched its character. However, all that remains here of the architecture of Wilhelm's reign is the Grotto Hall on the ground floor of the east wing – but it is impressive.

The Court was always a formal garden, subdivided into four equal sections. Unlike today's public gardens with their lawns and beech hedges, it boasted clearly demarcated gravel surfaces in the colours of the lozenge-patterned Bavarian coat-of-arms and en-

A Friedrich Sustris design for a ceiling painting in the (vanished) Grotto Hall west of the Grotto Court. In the drawing Phaeton is depicted asking Apollo for the chariot of Helios, the Sun.

closed by marble balustrades. The central feature of the Court, Hubert Gerhard's Perseus Fountain (1590), has been preserved. It is the symbolic key to understanding the entire complex. Perseus, son of Zeus and Danaë, was, like Hercules, a mythical figure of classical antiquity with whom the pious Wittelsbachs of the Late Renaissance identified themselves. Perseus' conquest of evil corresponded with the

The Grotto Court was designed (from 1583) as a sort of open-air festival hall. The sculpture decorating it refers to the myth of Perseus with the head of Medusa, whose glance turned those who saw it into stone.

Archangel Michael, hero and role model of the Counter Reformation. Gerhard had represented Michael just two years before as the patron saint of the new Jesuit church in Munich. The composition of this bronze derives from Benvenuto Cellini's famous group in the Florentine Loggia dei Lanzi. The Munich Field Marshal's Hall boasts a second cast of its own. In clothing the hero and rendering Medusa in a modest pose, Gerhard, however, arrived at an independent, less provocative solution.

Friedrich Sustris represented Perseus' victory over Medusa against a monumental scenic backdrop illustrating Medusa's magical powers of petrifying those who gazed on her. The sculptures arranged along the façades are, therefore, to be read as human victims of the Gorgon's Head. The overarching purpose of the composition was to convey an entirely new, realistic impression of the heroes of antiquity. No longer images of a long forgotten era, they represented human beings who had just ceased to breathe. Most of the marble sculptures unfortunately fell victim to the heavy Bavarian frosts; the remaining twelve are copies. Some of the originals today grace the Octagon Hall south of the Antiquarium.

The Architecture of the Grotto Hall

The Court's dominant motif is taken up in the barrel-vaulted Grotto Hall, which is closely linked with the open space by a graceful colonnade. The focal point of the Hall is a grotesque configuration, for which the term 'grotto' is not particularly apt. The five niches with fountain basins are more like that.

Sophisticated handling of the play of water and the use of spongy tufa, calcareous limestone and a variety of crystals reveal them as works of Italian Mannerist garden architecture. Three powerfully articulated façades decorated with coats of arms are highly distinctive. Their surfaces once shone in fairy-tale splendour with polished shells, marine molluscs, semiprecious stones and corals. It takes some time before one perceives the forms of birds, vases of flowers and all sorts of sea monsters made in the same way.

On the other hand, the central gilt bronze statue of Mercury underway with a message and modelled on Giambologna, is notable for exemplifying the Munich court style of the period.

Teeming with figures, human and animal, the Grotto architecture obviously seems to represent a more intimate treatment of petrified nature. It adds exuberance to the figures lining the court and emphasizes the free play of natural water and stone. The messenger of the gods is making straight for Perseus, bringing him tidings of the gods' approval of his heroic deed.

The Grotto Hall Painting

The vaulting of what has remained of the Grotto Hall once boasted magnificent gold highlights and painted grotesques. It was overspread with a light sky in which gods and goddesses disported themselves to create an effect of spaciousness in visual as well as ideal terms. Remains of paintings in the squinch arches are recognisably a sequence of scenes from Ovid's Metamorphoses. In the southern squinch a visit paid by Minerva to Mt Helicon is depicted. The assembled Muses tell of a song contest with women who paid for their audacity by being transformed into magpies. The story that follows it in Ovid's poetry is illustrated on the opposite side: here Minerva entered on a weaving contest with Arachne, a mortal. Arachne won and the envious goddess turned her into a spider. The back wall of the Grotto Hall also deals with the theme of transformation – after all, metamorphosis is the Greek word for it – in a sequence of four scenes to be read from left to right. In the first, Jupiter has transformed Io, one of the ladies he fancies, into a cow and Juno, mother of the gods, has charged Argus of the hundred eyes with guarding her. Mercury has put Argus to sleep at Jupiter's behest so that he can be killed. In the next scene Juno is depicted decorating her pea-

Detail of the Perseus Fountain in the Grotto Court. Hubert Gerhard made the Greek hero look like a knight versed in jousting; Medusa's severed head with its snaky locks lured the unwary even in death.

cock with the eyes of the faithless guard. Flying on, Mercury falls in love with pretty Herse, daughter of the king of Athens, when he spots her sacrificing to Minerva, surrounded by her maidens. The fourth painting narrates Mercury's revenge on Herse's sister, who was opposed to his wooing Herse: he turned her into a stone. The gilt statue of Mercury in the fountain alcove is thus woven into a fabric of references and allusions. Its contextual density of association and connotation is what makes the sculpture so important although, in some respect, the exciting Bologna model may be more refined.

The lower portion of the Grotto Hall is reserved for the sphere of all-too-human foibles. The motifs dealt with here are the pleasures of the natural life and exuberant joie de vivre. Hunting scenes on the narrow walls are references to this sport, then engaged in only by the aristocracy. Together with eight busts of such lesser wood deities as Paniskes, Satyrs and Sileni wreathed with vine leaves and set up on pedestals in alcoves along the wall, the hunting scenes lend a less serious touch to the mythological events depicted in the upper region. Here the actual purpose for which the gardens, pavilions and halls were built is addressed: they are places in which the luxury-loving court could seek relaxation, intellectual and sensuous enjoyment.

THE ANTIQUARIUM

In contrast to the playful Grotto Hall, the first impression here is one of amazement: a hall, seventy metres long, stretches in bays before the visitor, arch after arch discreetly lit by bull's-eye windows. Even though the dimensions of the Antiquarium (Room 7) date from Albrecht's reign, Friedrich Sustris was the one to accomplish the final effect, making it one of the supreme achievements of Renaissance art north of the Alps. As different as they are, the Grotto Hall and the Antiquarium complement each other. Creation in the raw transformed by heavenly powers is the theme of the Grotto Hall. The Antiquarium confronts it with the clearly articulated architecture of a state building spanning two millenia of Western culture. Its grandeur matches the new function of a ceremonial hall as the focus of state occasions. The collection of sculptures, representations of the most powerful rulers of antiquity which can be viewed as a cycle, symbolizes temporal power as

such. In this case it is the former duchy of Bavaria which is to be made aware of its good fortune in being under the benign Wittelsbach regime. The cycle of paintings of the Virtues gracing the vaulting soffits is an allegory of their rule.

View down the entire length of the Antiquarium to the main portal. Finished in 1600, the banquet hall of Duke Wilhelm V is one of the most splendid Renaissance rooms north of the Alps.

The Ceiling Paintings

The rather subdued colour scheme of the Antiquarium is due to damage sustained during the war. It had to be uniformly translated to the surfaces in

need of repainting. So skilful is the restoration that the difference can only be spotted when looking carefully – especially in the five central bays. The barrel vaulting between the seventeen cross vaults, which, looking along them, create an effect of alternating cuts with painted scenes continuing to the back of a stage, and, with the picture reserves all down the crown of the soffit, were originally conceived as a view up into the heavens. The effect desired was twofold: first, to raise the height of the room, which would otherwise seem rather squat and, second, to suggest the widening of intellectual and spiritual horizons to encompass the philosophical sphere remote from mundane concerns. Several pairs of putti (now only recognisable in sketchy outline) hover here, sporting various attributes symbolizing festivities of an elevated and edifying nature and especially, in a dialogue with the paintings in the crown of the soffit, harmony in a well regulated commonwealth.

Details of grotesques painted on the vaulted Antiquarium ceiling. A small castle (Haidau, south-east of Regensburg) is depicted in the window soffit, framed by bizarre wingèd beasts reminiscent of Hieronymus Bosch's fantastic creations.

The opulence of this painting, which covers a surface of more than eight hundred square metres, becomes apparent only gradually. It is revealed in the delicately articulated backgrounds which represent a world of bizarre mythical beings, realistically depicted animal and plant motifs, phiales smoking with incense and silky draperies. Yet again the weight of the vaulting is subverted. These grotesques, a type of ancient mural decoration rediscovered in Rome in about 1500, are related thematically to the busts of Roman emperors below them. It is well worth the effort to bring binoculars so that you can pick out the individual motifs, of which there are far more than a hundred.

The small-scale decoration ultimately leads into 102 vedute and landscapes embedded in them. Wilhelm V was committed to this project which, after several false starts, resulted in the creation of Hans Donauer's (*c.* 1521–96) late masterpiece. In oval reserves, the paintings are representations, often the earliest known, of familiar architectural landmarks and the landscapes surrounding thirty-four cities of the Duchy of Bavaria as well as its most important castles and market towns, rendered in faithful detail. The cultural landscape of Late Renaissance Bavaria is here in all its glory, presented with pride as the fruition of good government. In retrospect, however, it is astonishing how small the territory was which in 1600 formed the basis of the Wittelsbach cultural achievement.

The Allegories of the Virtues

The highest register of the Antiquarium pictorial language is represented by the paintings marking the crown of the soffit. Well preserved, they are the work of artists in Peter Candid's circle and were not long in replacing an earlier version. Based on ideas promulgated by Erasmus of Rotterdam, which in

The crown of the soffit is dominated by sixteen allegories of the Virtues. Here a painter from the circle of Peter Candid has personified the Christian virtue of charity as a mother surrounded by children.

turn go back to Cicero, the model of a Christian Humanist society is presented in eight oval and eight rectangular paintings. The allegorical female figures are surrounded by putti and accompanied by mottos on the adjacent vaulting.

The Christian virtues lead the procession, beginning with Faith (FIDES), Hope (SPES) and Charity (CARITAS), attesting to the piety of Wilhelm V. They are followed by the four Platonic cardinal virtues (Res. publ. 4: 227f) of Prudence (PRUDENTIA), Temperance (TEMPERANTIA), Justice (JUSTITIA) and Fortitude (FORTITUDO). The most comprehensive of these inaugurates the cycle as one of the large rectangular paintings. Beyond FAMA (Fame), at the centre, CONSTANTIA (Constancy or Steadfastness) represents a stabilizing countervailing force to Fortitude. With her book, VERITAS (Truth) incorporates

the Humanist ideal of education. Its basis forms a link back to Justice. The traits of Chastity (CASTITAS), Clemency (CLEMENTIA) and Patience (PATIENTIA), personified next to them, were handed down from antiquity. Humility (HUMILITAS), a very Christian virtue, has been added to their number. The sequence closes with ABSTINENTIA (Abstinence, implying incorruptibility) and OBOEDIENTIA (Obedience), moral categories applying to the civil servants of the state and, ultimately, including all subjects of the realm in the catalogue of virtues thus drawn up.

The Emperor Cycle

Jacobo Strada, renowned as the 'inventor' of the Antiquarium, published a work on numismatics in Zurich in 1557. Based on the Roman historian

Suetonius, it describes the Roman imperial families in succession. The rearrangement of the sculpture sequence in the Antiquarium, unique in its completeness, took this as a basis. It is subdivided into an upper row of consorts of Roman emperors and a lower one comprising the Roman emperors. On the left, above the main entrance, the central axes of the first three windows are dedicated to the numerous women who played a role in Gaius Julius Caesar's life. The wives, daughters and maternal ancestors of Augustus, Julius Caesar's grand nephew and the first Roman Emperor, go up to the fifth window. The Julian-Claudian line continues until the twelfth window, closing fittingly with Nero's wives: Octavia, Poppaea and Messalina the Younger. The female Flavians are represented by the wives of the four emperors who succeeded each other in the violent year 69 AD: Galba, Otho, Vitellius and Vespasian.

The east side which follows is devoted first to the ladies in the circle of the adopted Antonine emperors, Antoninus Pius, Marcus Aurelius and Lucius Verus, and then those of the line of Severus, which was succeeded in 235 AD by the turbulent era of the Soldier Emperors. The family of Constantine I the Great rounds off the cycle of imperial Roman ladies. Constantine's conversion to Christianity in 320 initiated the era of Christian rule with which the Late Renaissance felt a close affinity.

The sequence is less consistently ordered in the lower row, where the busts of the men who held power in the Roman Empire are named. The first twelve rulers from Julius Caesar to the Emperor Domitian are dealt with in the first six axes of the hall. The long wall concludes with Valerian, who ruled until 260 AD. Now we have reached the age of the Soldier Emperors. The east side begins, to the right of the main entrance, as it should, with figures from the Roman Republic but soon the sequence is no longer consistent.

Knowledgeable visitors will note considerable contradictions between the portraits and the names they bear. Gaps in knowledge at the time when the busts were made, losses and changes made over the past four centuries may be the reason for the confusion. Between Julius Caesar and Septimus Severus (d. 211), that is, the great age of the Roman Empire, the great majority of Emperors and some members of their families are on display in authentic portrait busts, ten of which are even correctly labelled.

The Sculpture in the Antiquarium

Evaluating the sculpture which is above the labelled ledges along the wall and in the niches of the piers is equally problematic. Quite a few are in a state of preservation comparable with that of works in modern collections. Archeological expertise was not available when the pieces were found. Restoration work was often makeshift and transport by ox-cart did not help to ensure the safety of these fragile works of ancient sculpture. Elaborate bust pieces made in Bavaria filled in gaps to provide historical continuity by furnishing the ancient heads, most of which were notable for their severe simplicity, with a stable base to create an effect of similarity and imperial dignity. The most important sculptor active in adding busts to the ancient heads was Hans Ernhofer (d. 1621), who was rediscovered only recently. Two thirds of the roughly 270 pieces displayed in the Antiquarium are, essentially, genuine works of venerated antiquity. The remaining third is equally divided between Renaissance sculpture and works from the eighteenth and nineteenth centuries.

Even though the overall impression is one of monumentality, it is worthwhile taking a closer look at individual pieces. Some notable works are the statues of youths on the wall of the

Part of the Antiquarium wall, elevation drawn by Johann Mathias Kager, 1611. The drawing is evidence that the interior decoration has hardly changed. The recent reconstruction of the windows is based on this drawing.

portal: to the left, a generously restored ancient Apollo and, to the right, a late Hellenistic torso wearing a light cloak. A Greek head of Hermes has been fittingly added to it. This figure has been viewed as a Renaissance idea of David. Well matched by Apollo, god of the arts and light, the statue of the Old Testament hero and singer and its companion-piece are attuned to the festive atmosphere of the room. After all, the court musicians had their place near the portal.

A head of Julius Caesar opens the series of busts. In excellent condition, it

The staggered effect created by its deep bays is apparent when the Antiquarium is seen from an angle. An exuberant realm of grotesque creatures and plants on the Italian model emerges to subvert the stringent ordering of the sculpture below it.

was probably not made until about 1800 and was modelled on a work in Pisa.

Above this bust and slightly off centre is the earliest piece in the collection, a little head of a severe-looking woman. She is Calpurnia, Julius Caesar's third wife. Probably provincial Greek, the work dates from the mid-5th century AD.

Diana, goddess of hunting, possibly by the Venetian sculptor Jacopo Sansovino. This is one of the finest of the fourty-one late Renaissance busts in the Antiquarium.

Under the fourth window, the bust of a corpulent man with a distinctive face is a striking Baroque sculpture. Modelled on a Venetian work, it was long regarded as a 'Vitellius', Nero's immediate successor, and bears his label. However, the portrait of the last Claudian Emperor is displayed on the bottom row of the opposite side, on the left under the sixth window.

Progressing down the hall, stop just before the great stair to look at a charming portrait of a girl with a headful of curls. Comparison with Venetian sculpture suggests that this is a work from Jacopo Sansovino's circle (1486–1570). If so, it exemplifies sculpture dating from the time the collection was started and shares the provenance of most of the collection.

The last pier but one before the chimney boasts a nude sculpture of a youth with a cloak flung over his shoulders who is holding an amphora. Despite serious damage to an arm and the legs and crude additions to the head, the high quality of the torso is unmistakable. This is a Greek work from the Parthenon period (*c.* 450 BC).

Across from it, on a pedestal, is a replica of the Aphrodite of Aphrodisias, one of at least twenty-eight replicas of this Hellenistic cult statue. It is among the most famous ancient sculptures acquired by Albrecht. This copy probably dates from the first half of the second century AD.

The Antiquarium Furniture and the Room's Function as a Banqueting Hall

Even after 1600 the Antiquarium was still a museum. However, it only really came alive when festivities were staged in it. Usually furnished on a temporary basis, it did boast a few stationary pieces which are interesting as the earliest extant furnishings of the Residence.

The custom of the imperial court required that diners assembled here looked at a enclosed dais reserved for the hosts and their highest-ranking guests. The royal banquet table still stood on this dais in the nineteenth century. Its scagliola (coloured plaster imitating marble) top was one of the earliest of its kind extant. The table was moved to the Stone Rooms and was destroyed in 1944. However, two original walnut credenzas are still in place at the side of the fireplace in the Antiquarium. Magnificent pieces from banquet services were displayed on them. The specialists in fine carving focused on rosettes and mascarons. They may have been the creators of the choir pews in St Michael's Church. The lower zone of the credenzas, which are built-in, can be opened across the full front to reveal a number of shallow drawers where silver and dishes used on the court table may have been stored or, and this is more likely, Kunstkammer pieces were displayed.

The two credenzas and perhaps all the Antiquarium appointments would have been removed to make room for newer furnishings if the hall had been suitable for banqueting. It had the drawback of being almost impossible to heat (the city palace was used mainly in the cold seasons of the year). Moreover, the approach to it did not accommodate the festive processions which were so popular then. It was soon replaced as the banqueting hall by the Hercules Hall because it was centrally located and the Imperial Hall, which was planned from the outset as a room for state occasions. The Antiquarium was downgraded to the status of curiosity cabinet, in fact, a sort of room for storing what was not needed elsewhere. This is why it has been pre-

The Antiquarium fireplace bears the date it was finished: MDC–1600–*and the name of the man who completed it: Duke Maximilian I.*

served almost as it was. Recent restoration has reinserted the original fenestration with its soft light. The room's museum function has been re-emphasized and important guests are even occasionally received here, just as they were in 1600.

One of a pair of credenzas (sideboards) in the window alcoves at the north end of the Antiquarium. Like the princely table that once stood here, they were essential requisites of banquet ceremony. These are the earliest original pieces of furniture still in the Residence.

Court Garden tract:
110 The Hall of the Four Greys
111 Imperial Hall
112 Imperial Stair

Stone Rooms Tract:
104 Room of the Church, 105 Room of Religion,
106 Room of Eternity, 107 Room of the Seasons,
108 Room of the World, 109 Room of the Elements,
114 Theatiner Corridor

Trier Rooms:
47 Hall of the Prince, 53 Hall of the Council

The Court Chapels:
89 Court Chapel, 98 Rich Chapel

Collection Rooms:
91, 92, 93 First, Second and Third Sacred Vestments Rooms

Isometric projection of the Court Chapel complex and the Imperial Court tracts

Main façade in Residenz Strasse, finished in 1616. The marble portal with bronze statues from Hans Krumper's workshop stands out as a bold touch of plasticity against the painted columns.

Rooms from the Period of Maximilian I (1598–1651)

EXTERNAL APPEARANCE

The Main Façade on Residenz Strasse

The main façade of the complex, dating from the reign of Maximilian I, still looks much as it did then and is its distinctive feature. The west front, which is 150 metres long, has lost some of its original monumentality through more recent additions. The two marble portals decorated with sculpture convey an idea of Maximilian's world of thought. The pediment of the northern Imperial Gate is occupied by Wisdom personified, reading and guiding the government. Her companion-piece is Justice, with a radiant sun yet menacing with the Roman fasces. The Chapel Gate in the south still boasts its sumptuously mounted original door wings. Above it Fortitude is armed

with a Herculean cudgel. The rock keeps assault at bay. Her companion-piece, Temperance, commands regulated conduct of affairs, symbolized by a clock. Four faithful guardian lions explain the symbols with shields sporting reliefs. Although originally commissioned by Wilhelm V from Hubert Gerhard and Carlo Pallago for a funerary monument, they now put Munich in a good mood; rubbing the shiny grotesque noses of the lion mascarons at the bottom of the shields brings good luck.

The most important façade sculpture is Hans Krumper's (*b.* Weilheim, *c.* 1570–1634) 'Patrona Boiariae', a youthful yet motherly personification of Bavaria. Madonna-like, she holds the Christ Child on her arm, his hand raised in blessing the country. The Latin inscription on the cartouche surmounting the sculpture can be translated as 'We flee under your protective shield, where we live in security and

A performance in the Residence Fountain Court, a popular summer venue for jazz, classical music and fringe theatre.

the court chapel here, of which only two arched windows beside the portal are visible. We move on to encounter a charming relic of chivalry: a stone chained to the ground surmounted by a plaque with three nails. Christoph, Duke of Bavaria (1449–93), an adventurer and rebel, was famous for his physical prowess and agility. Passers-by are invited to compete with him by lifting the stone and jumping as high as the third nail. 'He who leaps higher,' runs the text, 'will also achieve renown.'

Enclosing the Bavarian Dukes' old tournament grounds, the elongated Fountain Court now provides a romantic setting for open-air concerts. Until the covered passages were built, the doughty Neuveste was the dominant

happiness'. The date the work was finished – MDCXVI or 1616 – is on the marble niche. The monumental painted pilasters articulating the stuccoed façade fade into the background behind the handsome bronze sculptures. The painting was reconstructed by 1958 on simplified lines after the collapsed upper floors had been rebuilt.

The Renaissance Court

Renovated by 1980, the Imperial Court similarly exemplifies contemporary wall design based on an historic original. Reached via the Western Portal, the Imperial Court once saw processions of important state visitors. Here stringent geometry contrasted sharply with the untidily labyrinthine city. The west tract had to be wedge-shaped to fit into the street plan. The court surface, comprising 'a day's work' (when it was laid out, fields were measured in terms of the time it took to till them), is impressive by any standards, royal or otherwise.

The South Gate leads into the bare Chapel Court, which was once the Jägergassl (Hunter's Lane) in the town. The name of the space derives from

One of four guardian lions along the Residence west façade. Originally made by Hubert Gerhard (c. 1594) as heraldic elements of a monumental tomb planned by Duke Wilhelm V.

The nave of the Court Chapel, consecrated in 1601 and resembling the only slightly earlier Jesuit church of St Michael. With its massive barrel vaulting St Michael's broke new ground in Baroque architecture north of the Alps.

landmark to the east. The higher roofs along the west side conceal the Antiquarium tract. The pediments were added to the gabled ends towards 1612 to mark the new main entrances to the palace. The southern end of the Fountain Court affords a delightful view of the intricate windings of the complex with the clock tower (rebuilt by 1958) soaring above them.

The court was named after the fountain at its centre. The chief sculpture is a representation of Otto, Duke of Bavaria, the first ruler of the Wittelsbach dynasty. The framing groups of sculpture include personifications of the elements and all sorts of nautical personages from an earlier context. Hubert Gerhard's workshop finished the fountain and its sculpture as it is today in 1613.

THE COURT CHAPEL (Hofkapelle) AND THE RICH CHAPEL (Reiche Kapelle)

The Court Chapel

Maximilian, Duke of Bavaria, especially worshipped the Virgin Mary, and this is shown in the 'Patrona Boiariae' taking up the centre of the main Residence façade and the Virgin's Column at the heart of his capital city. In this spirit, the Court Chapel (Room 89) was renovated from 1600 and consecrated to the Virgin. The stark white interior of the chapel recalls St Michael's Church, which was finished shortly before the chapel. However, the barrel vaulting of the chapel is much more densely encrusted with stucco decoration. Hans Krumper

Double page overleaf: The clock tower above the Fountain Court marks the centre of the palace. Hubert Gerhard's fountain in the foreground commemorates Otto I, founder of the Wittelsbach dynasty, with groups of allegorical figures.

arranged Marian symbols expressing praise of the Queen of Heaven round the central logogriph for the Virgin's name. The chancel vault (1630: the court surrounding the chapel was not covered over until then by a room for a new altar) continues the theme in the same style. This part of the room was rebuilt after World War II; the decoration of the main chapel room, saved with great difficulty, is, therefore, especially precious. From the passages around it, which open in three rows of arches into the church, the Bavarian Court attended divine service daily. The social position of each member of the Court was shown in the place reserved for him or her just as it would be later in the Baroque Theatre.

The chapel appointments are quite simple. Originally gilt, the High Altar dominates the room. The central panel shows the Virgin, enthroned in front of choirs of angels. At her feet, in the zone representing earthly concerns, noble ladies have gathered in prayer. Both groups of figures are focused on the Holy Trinity, which can be found on top of the altarpiece. The painter was Hans Werl, whose abilities were long underestimated. Like his contemporary Peter Candid, he belonged to the circle of Friedrich Sustris. The two side altars (1748), framed by Rococo stucco with paintings of Saints Anne and Maximilian, are the work of Johann Baptist Zimmermann and his son, Franz Michael.

Scagliola plaque from the Rich Chapel with a motif from the Life of the Virgin. Wilhelm Fistulator, whose family held a monopoly on scagliola, created this and nine other stucco intarsia panels.

The High Altar of the Rich Chapel, finished in about 1615. Used for the Wittelsbachs' private devotions, the chapel was also a repository of holy relics they collected.

The Rich Chapel

By far the most sumptuous place of worship in the complex, the Rich Chapel (Reiche Kapelle, Room 98) was reserved for the private devotions of Maximilian I and the members of his immediate family. The central position of this chapel is typical of Catholic Court practice: the focal point of the two suites of ducal apartments, the bedchamber of the duke and duchess abutted it to the south. From the adjacent gallery one looked down into the Court Chapel. Above the portal stands the date the Rich Chapel was consecrated: 1607. The main function of this small room with its domed ceiling was to hold the treasure of relics which is now exhibited separately in the Residence Museum. The unique spiritual powers attributed to these devotional memorabilia was to be matched by the unprecedented splendour of their ar-

chitectural setting, designed by Hans Krumper. The dominant feature of the Rich Chapel is its wall decoration of scagliola plaques of a type which would later decorate other rooms in the Residence. Now they are again limited to this chapel. A technique of colouring multi-faceted stucco intarsia so that it could take a marble-like polished finish, scagliola was developed from the late sixteenth century in the Munich Residence, at first for use in furniture decoration. Blasius Pfeiffer, also called Blasius Fistulator, invented this type of scagliola, for which he and his heirs were granted a ducal monopoly. The next generation saw Wilhelm Fistulator create figurative motifs like the lavish vases of flowers in the Rich Chapel. The supreme achievement of artisans working in this technique is a series of ten scenes from the Life of the Virgin after Albrecht Dürer. They were embedded in the long wall in 1632 as a votive offering in gratitude for the departure of the Swedes, who had occupied Munich. Recalling exquisite watercolours, these scagliola pictures make one forget that each colour tone corresponds to a layer of stucco laid on separately and polished to achieve it. Six of the motifs, all of them on the wall with the window, are originals. The reconstruction of the others and the revival of this almost forgotten art is one of the great feats of post-war rebuilding.

Painted with precious azurite dust, the deep blue domed ceiling overarches the sacred room like a night sky. Its gilt reliefs, pieced together again from fragments, narrate events from the Lives of Christ, the Virgin and the Saints.

Once oppressively packed with furnishings, the Chapel was cleared out as early as 1937, when it was opened to the public as part of the Museum. A trinity of essentials remains: the original High Altar, the elaborate organ and (unfortunately, only the richly decorated front), the matching reliquary. Old pieces were used to construct all of them. The twelve-tiered ebony altar, delivered in 1605 by the Munich artist Paulus Dietrich, is, although quite small, a monumental work. Only a closer look reveals the sumptuousness of its silver reliefs, which illustrate the theme of the monarchy with examples from the Old Testament. The central plaque, a Crucifixion relief by Jakob Anthoni of Augsburg, could be lowered to reveal the most precious piece in the collection of relics, a monstrance now in the Reliquary Room (see illus. p. 111).

The solemn grandeur of dark browns and silver recurs in the instrument on the window wall. In addition, the tripartite organ case glitters with hundreds of engraved stones, enamelled gold scales and miniature paintings on ivory. The exquisitely chased pipes are, by the way, just for show. A hidden mechanism might have been heard in their place. The reliquary across from it is notable for its delicately engraved glass reliefs. Creating such a flawlessly transparent artificial material represented an outstanding technical achievement in 1590. Zacharias Pelzer's reliefs have a great deal of depth. Like the relics once housed in this monstrance, they relate to the Crucifixion.

THE IMPERIAL COURT TRACTS

The Court Garden Tract with the Imperial Stair and Imperial Hall

Adolf Feulner, an art historian, wrote about the 'web of profound yet tangled erudition' which he saw covering the appointments of the rooms discussed in the following. Their original significance and the philosophies underlying them have been for the most part forgotten. However, if you regard all the pleasingly arranged cycles of paintings, tapestries, stucco reliefs and bandaroles merely as dazzling interior decoration, you miss something essential. We are still able to trace the overarching themes, at least sketchily. Maximilian, hitherto Duke of Bavaria, became Prince Elector in 1623, and, apart from his pronounced religious zeal, was a great visionary and erudite monarch, who wanted the construction of his palace to be understood as his legacy to a politics of high moral standing.

The main approach to the Imperial Court tracts, finished in 1616, is on the north side of the Imperial Court. The Hall of Four Pillars (Vierschäftesaal) is the first room visitors enter to reach the large reception rooms on the main floor. Since it lost its painted ceilings in the war, the Hall of Four Pillars is rather simple today and forms the anteroom to the State Collection of Egyptian Art. The area is not accessible directly from the Residence Museum. However, the description follows the route taken by the grand processions of Maximilian's day.

The Imperial Stair, finished in about 1616, in the Court Garden tract. The effect of spaciousness and light it created on the main floor was an architectural feature, unusual for the time, which anticipated the broad stairwells of the Baroque period.

The Imperial Stair (Kaisertreppe, Room 112) is a prelude to revolutionary architecture. It is not only a direct link between the floors; it also provides a platform for lofty themes like the rise and fall of ambitious kings, the passage of time or the ascent from benighted oppression to the sun of enlightened monarchy. The journey in the heavens undertaken by the demigod Hercules (a symbol of power in Bavarian mythology) figures prominently in the vaulting of the first flight whereas the fall of Icarus warns of the dangers of hybris in the second flight. Hans Krumper's statues of monarchs present the Wittelsbachs in person. However, the founder of the dynasty, Otto I, and its most successful scion, the Emperor Ludwig the Bavarian, are linked with Charlemagne by a flight of historical fancy resulting from rivalry with the House of Habsburg. Reconstructed by Karl Manninger by 1975, the narrative painting in the vaulting is capricious in tone and grotesque in style.

Having been put in the mood for a special experience, you enter the Imperial Hall (Kaisersaal, Room III), which is thirty-four metres long. The gilt ceiling is nearly 10 metres above the floor and the walls are covered with paintings and tapestries. The Imperial Hall as you see it is a creation of the 1980s. Details of decoration, the choice of materials used and the lighting were subject to various constraints; yet important furnishings, put into storage in 1800, have been returned to their original context to restore a feeling of meaningful continuity. The central ceiling painting, which was also the semantic focus of the hall, was lost during the war. Now it is represented by large coloured photos. The oval central reserve represents Fame, personified in the radiant figure of an angel, as the prize for which a virtuous ruler should strive. The other two main fields contain (at the entrance) personifications of Wisdom, a matron with the symbolic representations of the Seven Liberal Arts and (at the fireplace) Power, represented by the four kingdoms of antiquity. Their inevitable end stands as a warning to their successors. Circles of smaller paintings filled with putti engaged in relevant activities elucidate each of the above. The entire cycle was painted by Peter Candid's workshop (c. 1548–1628), familiar to the visitor from the Antiquarium.

The ceiling frieze contains a sequence of paintings by Andrea Michieli, called Vicentino, a Venetian artist. Two heroic cycles confront virtuous deeds from the Bible (on the north side) with parallels from classical mythology (on the south side). Twelve tapestries, covering nearly half the open space of the walls, have been hung round the piers below. Related to the panel paintings, they too record virtuous deeds, in this instance alternately those performed by men and women. Designed by Peter Candid, the tapestries were woven in Enghien, France (completed by 1618). Today, a selection fills the blocked-up windows along the north side of the hall.

The niche on the chimney breast, which echoes the form of the main entrance, once contained a porphyry-coloured stucco statue of Virtue. The way it looked was recently discovered when a sketch dating from about 1680 came to light. Now Hubert Gerhard's Tellus Bavarica, personifying the country of Bavaria and its riches, stands in its place, a work which was copied from the roof of the Court Garden temple (see illus. p. 5).

The Imperial Hall has assumed many of the functions which once

One of the largest state rooms in the Residence until 1800, the Imperial Hall was reconstructed and completed in 1985 and is now again its most popular event venue.

proved too much for the Antiquarium and its less robust appointments, yet another good reason for turning architectural history back by 185 years.

The Stone Rooms and the Hall of the Four Greys

The next suite of rooms, the Stone Rooms (Steinzimmer), was named after its costly stone floors. Approached

through the Hall of the Four Greys, the Stone Rooms were the most elegant visitors' accommodation at the disposal of the Bavarian Electors. The last person to live in them was Luitpold, the Prince Regent, who stayed here until his death in 1912. The names of the rooms match the themes of their ceiling paintings. Even though more than fifty per cent of the paintings were lost in the war, and large-scale replacement had been necessary after the fire of

1674, the content of the iconographic programme can still be reconstructed.

The 'Four Greys', which gave their name to the first room (Room 110), stand for the team that drew the chariot of the sun in the centre field of the ceiling which is now empty. Personifications of four (once six) planets indicate that the room itself signified the universe. The adjacent Room of the Elements (Room 109) boasts representations of the elements, the winds and the seasons of the year, all of which affect the uninhabited earth–in the antechamber reserve. The next room, the Room of the World (Room 108) sports all sorts of beasts circling about a centre which, until 1944, was occupied by an allegory of man as the conqueror of nature. In contrast to the ceilings of the adjacent rooms that have been constructed in wood, the ceiling of the smaller middle room of the Stone Room suite, the Four Seasons Room (Room 107), has been stuccoed and painted. The theme is time, subdivided into sidereal, seasonal and monthly cycles. Time also plays a leading role in the system of the planets, which is also depicted. The next three rooms to the south (104–106) invade the sphere of philosophy with the themes of eternity, religion and the Church (the Roman Catholic Church) Triumphant. Looking back to the Imperial Hall, one has to admire this grand scheme of universal order which includes everything visible and imaginable.

The portals and chimney-breast niches dating from 1700 were reconstructed by 1973 from fragments. Dealing with more mundane concerns, their decoration in scagliola-style is nonetheless technically sophisticated.

Tapestries and Furniture in the Stone Rooms

The tapestries are the greatest treasure in the Stone Rooms. Ten of these, woven after designs by Peter Candid, are outstanding. Even though the dyes are not lightfast, scenes from the life of Otto I, Duke of Bavaria, have been preserved in all the rich splendour of their original colours because these hangings were only brought out on very special occasions. Now they have to be protected from sunlight by special shades. The broad borders of the tapestries, decorated with the arms of the ducal family and clusters of trophies, clarify the iconographic programme of the scenes in Latin texts. The achievements of the founder of the Wittelsbach dynasty, brought about by his skilful diplomacy, are illustrated with sweeping pictures. Two key scenes in the Four Seasons Room are particularly noteworthy: Otto's crafty attacks saved Emperor Barbarossa's army in 1155 from invasion by Verona. A second tapestry shows Otto's reward: being raised to Duke of Bavaria in 1180.

By the sixteenth century the Munich court was buying tapestries from the Netherlands such as the Hercules tapestries from what is now the Residence concert hall. Maximilian was so fond of tapestries, in his day the most elaborate form of wall decoration, that he even wanted to supervise the making of the finest pieces personally. To satisfy his whim, up to twenty specialist craftsmen were kept at work in the Residence between 1604 and 1615 under the supervision of the Brussels master Hans van der Biest. Maximilian preferred smooth, very closely woven tapestries dyed in durable colours. The materials for them, wool and silk thread of various qualities, were bought in Antwerp. The most precious material used in making these tapestries was thread wound round with gold or silver and it came from Italy.

The cost of such labour-intensive and time-consuming work is said to have been astronomical. Now for a few figures. The mean amount of work a tapestry-maker did per month was 0.44 square metres, that means a team of three men had to work three to four

The Stone Rooms adjacent to the Imperial Hall were a suite reserved for the most important guests. Bavaria's last monarch but one, Luitpold the Prince Regent, lived here. The carefully restored marbled stucco portals were erected after the fire of 1674.

Tapestry from the twelve-part Otto von Wittelsbach cycle in the Stone Rooms, signed by Hans van der Biest (1611). They depict deeds performed by the founder of the dynasty, here a ride to inspect the founding of the city of Landshut (which was really founded by Otto's son).

A detail of the above. A closer look reveals the extreme precision with which the silk tapestry was worked. It owes its brilliance to lavish use of gold thread.

weeks to make a square metre of tapestry, which contained about 3000 rows of thread. A medium-sized tapestry cost 1250 guilders, four years' wages for a master craftsman.

Most of the furniture from Maximilian's palace has been lost; the furnishings and appointments of these rooms are, therefore, of more recent date. A notable exception is a centre table of uncertain provenance, which is now in the Room of the Seasons. This piece

um. The top sports the Electoral coat of arms of Bavaria and must, therefore, have been made after 1623. It is the work of Wilhelm Fistulator, the 'Marmorator' or scagliola-maker. In the Room of Religion, not too far off, there is another octagonal table-top in pietra-dura, a technique by means of which mosaics were made of marble and semiprecious stones. It was introduced in Munich from Florence shortly before 1600. As hard as crystal, the

Centre table from the Four Seasons Room. Hans Ernhofer, the creator of many busts in the Antiquarium, made the base support (c. 1675); the scagliola top by Wilhelm Fistulator was made five decades later.

was created over different periods. The foot of the table is of polished walnut. Three lion paws alternate with winged mythical beings, a skilful variation on Italian models. The base support is attributed to Hans Ernhofer, a late 16th-century sculptor whose work we have already encountered in the Antiquari-

best of native Bavarian scagliola work surpasses the Italian pietra-dura in its appearance. The surfaces are seamless, the ornamental patterning exquisite and the palette rich and uniformly brilliant.

The Hall of the Prince of the Trier Rooms. The antechamber to an audience hall shows important paintings by Peter Candid. The walls are hung with a tapestry cycle of the Four Seasons designed by the same artist.

The Trier Rooms (Trierzimmer)

Two other suites of apartments for visitors were designed symmetrically on the east side of the Imperial Court. They could be reached via the Imperial Stair through the White Hall or via the Broad Stair near the (old) Hercules Hall. The covered passage along the back, which was later fenestrated in

the neo-classical style, was yet another approach. The modern name of these suites goes back to a Prince-Bishop of Trier, who often stayed here as a guest in the late eighteenth century. The three rooms in the centre were often renovated. After World War II, they were refurbished in the simplified fashion of their original construction. Originally, however, it was not possible to look through all interconnecting rooms. The rooms at the both ends of the wing, consisting of a large antechamber and a smaller audience chamber each, are still impressive examples of the style Maximilian cultivated. The old name of 'Royal Rooms' referred to the overarching theme of the ceiling paintings, which are among the most exuberant and exquisitely painted achievements of the Candid Workshop.

We shall have to restrict ourselves here to the first room to the south, the Hall of the Prince (Saal des Fürsten, Room 47). More than any other the Hall of the Prince bears the master's signature. PRINCEPS, the Prince, is enthroned in the centre of the ceiling.

The soldiers and men of law peering out from behind the baldachin recur in the two round paintings to the north, here accompanied by the attributes of their professions. On the window side, the companion-piece to the Rule of Law is an idyllic rendering of a loving couple. On the other side, War is depicted in a sombre battle-piece. Read as a whole, the captions translate as: 'The ruler not only arms himself with weapons but also with a strong state of law so that he can govern properly in war and peace.' The smaller paintings in the stucco frieze designed by Hans Krumper represent running commentaries on this core statement.

The extreme realism of this pictorial language is taken up in the tapestry cy-

Ceiling painting from the Hall of the Prince: peaceful idylls contrast with military motifs in another round painting.

cle which adorns the four rooms discussed in more detail here. A sequence of the twelve months, it was made in Bavaria after preliminary drawings by Peter Candid. Here we encounter people who lived in the seventeenth century: peasants, the mercantile classes and the nobility, all meticulously depicted as engaged month by month in the pursuits typical of their respective stations in life. As if from a pergola, you gaze out at this sweeping panorama of a vanished society. The naturalistic faces, distant views of familiar city landmarks and even occasional eye contact with the people so lovingly

Detail of a pair of cabinets with tortoiseshell marquetry by Johann Georg Esser and Wolfbauer. The Prince Elector Maximilian Emmanuel (1662–1726) acquired them in 1680 for his redecorated apartments.

Rural scene from the tapestry for the month of March in the Trier Rooms. Designed by Peter Candid and made by the court workshops.

portrayed leave the spectator strangely moved.

A notable suite of exquisite furniture is noteworthy, matching the stately magnificence of the Trier Rooms quite well even though these pieces came from a different setting. The Prince Elector Max Emmanuel had the two tables and cabinets-on-stands made in 1680/85 by the Augsburg cabinet-makers Esser and Wolfbauer for his new reception and drawing-rooms. A cabinet is in the Hall of the Prince and the other pieces are in the Hall of the Council (Room 53).

The glossy chequered surface of this furniture consists in tortoiseshell veneer on a red ground. The veneer in turn is inlaid with scrollwork interspersed with floral and animal motifs. The different materials, including mother of pearl, copper, brass and silver, create an effect of changing light and colour. Details are rendered in exquisitely delicate engraving. The marquetry technique used here, anticipating Boulle-work, highlights the contrast between surfaces and cut-out parts in identical patterns which, as far as colour is concerned, are positives and negatives. We are particularly fortunate in being able to see two such pairs of cabinets made at the same time in one workshop.

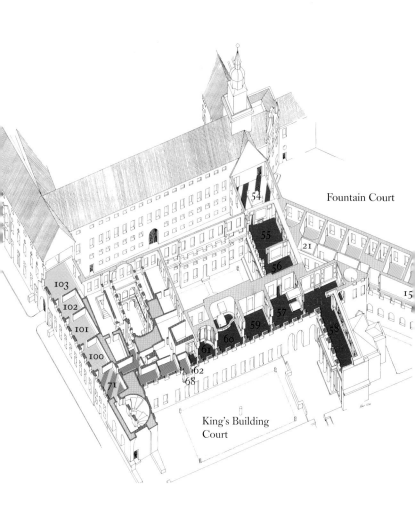

Electoral Rooms

Rich Rooms:
55 Antechamber, 56 Outer Audience Room, 57 Inner Audience Room,
58 Green Gallery, 59 Conference Room, 60 State Bedroom,
61 Mirror Cabinet, 62 Cabinet of Miniatures

Papal Chambers:
68 Heart Cabinet, 71 Golden Hall

Collection Rooms:
100–103 Court plate, 15–21 East Asian Collection

Isometric projection of the Papal and Rich Rooms

Baroque Rooms
(1665–1737)

THE PAPAL ROOMS

The Vanished Apartments of the Electresses

In 1665, Henriette-Adelaide of Savoy (1636–76), the wife of Ferdinand Maria, the Prince Elector of Bavaria, finally moved into the apartments previously occupied by her late mother-in-law. This meant that the rooms of the Residence, considered as one overall work of art, were enriched in a number of respects. Politically ambitious, the Electress was finally able to create a personal environment for herself and her descendents, which for the first time rivalled that enjoyed by the Elector. In introducing the Italian High Baroque style to Bavaria, she paved the way for her country's new style and greatly developed the iconographic programme of the Residence by taking up where Maximilian I had left off. The terrible fire of 1944 destroyed much of what she achieved.

The staircase which is now at the core of Henriette's apartment was not constructed in this period; although modelled on one dating from 1600, it was actually built in 1958. This is just one of a number of later additions to have hindered reconstruction of the suite as it was in the Electress' day. The heavy grandeur of Italianate Baroque was not appreciated in the 1950s, when Rococo was more in favour. Apart from the Heart Cabinet, therefore, only a handful of recently re-allocated doors, the overdoors and some remains of the ceiling panelling recall the vanished interiors. Moreover, the name 'Papal Chambers', which the suite has borne since a visit by Pope Pius VI in 1782, has obscured its earlier function and most important occupant.

Fortunately, major parts of the iconographic programme have been preserved. The Electress, a well-read woman, planned it together with the Marchese Ranuccio Sforza Pallavicino, a cleric from Parma. His description of it, which was published at that time, has clarified many uncertain points.

The Golden Hall, an audience chamber, finished off the Electress' rooms of state (Room 71). It is now part of the Court Plate exhibition (see p. 117). Apart from the frieze, the cycle of paintings has been preserved, albeit in a ceiling reconstructed on simplified lines. Numerous historic encounters between rulers and their subjects are represented here. Typical of Henriette's style, they appeal for tolerance and the accountability of the person in power. They were painted by Johann Heinrich Schönfeld.

The ceiling paintings which once adorned the adjacent sitting-room, called the Grotto Chamber because of a shell-trimmed wall fountain in it, have been moved to the Red Chamber (Room 67). A hymn of praise to Henriette-Adelaide has been adapted into

The Electress, Henriette-Adelaide of Savoy, energetically promoted the Italian style at the Munich court. A portrait from the Residence Portrait Gallery, workshop of Georges Desmarées, after 1730.

the well-known motif of the Wittels-bach virtues, underlining their high ambitions. Two life-size portraits on the wall, although rather formulaic, acquaint us with the personalities of Elector Ferdinand Maria, a melancholy man, and his vivacious and energetic wife. Nothing remains of the furnishings of 1670; most pieces now on display date from the early eighteenth century.

The royal bedchamber with stage-like alcoves which was once here, was the most magnificent room in the suite. Antonio Triva painted the ceiling decoration, which is yet another allegorical celebration of the Electress' capacity for steadfastness, wisdom, fortitude and friendship. It is now in the Green Chamber (Room 69) to the west.

The Heart Cabinet (Herzkabinett)

A rare exception to all this lost grandeur is Henriette-Adelaide's most intimate private room, the Heart Cabinet (Room 68), which is almost unchanged. The scagliola wall panelling was, however, destroyed and has been replaced with green silk. When comparing Johann Pader's ceiling panelling, the most important decorative element of the cabinet, with the meticulous execution of works created under Maximilian, a degree of uncertainty in the handling of new forms can be seen. Nonetheless, the uniform gold tone of the room smooths over any discrepancies in details. The heart motif reigns supreme, coupled with the recurrent so-called love-knot. These motifs represent the insignia of a military order originally formed under the name of the Knights of the Annunciade, to which the members of the House of Savoy belonged. The horse and lion, ridden by putti, are devices of the royal families, allied in marriage, which are also represented by coats of arms.

Caspar Amort, who executed the ceiling paintings, was commissioned to express Love in various guises without, however, offending his patroness' strict

Bedchamber of the Electress Henriette-Adelaide of Savoy in the Papal Chambers. Only a handful of paintings (in Room 69) have been preserved from this, the most magnificent room in the suite. Its Italianate Baroque splendour comes to life in a tinted print dating from 1880.

Ceiling of the Heart Cabinet in the Papal Chambers. The allegorical paintings after motifs from novels are attributed to Caspar Amort.

notions of morality. He therefore made his putti appear with their typical attributes while giving some of them peculiar ones. The central painting shows a wreath of little angels circling the hearts of the electoral couple, which are pierced with an arrow. Central to the sense of the painting is the symbolic meaning of the flowers depicted which would have been clearly inter-

preted by Henriette's contemporaries. The putti playing with tortured hearts in the diagonal axes of the room and the other fields of the ceiling evoke painful aspects of marital fidelity and intimacy.

The pictorial idiom of the cabinet is distilled to its essence in the three main paintings of the frieze. The painting on the wall next to the door is a representation of a 'City of Friendship'. This imagery is elucidated on the chimney-breast, which sports a quotation from Madeleine de Scudéry's romance *Clélie* in the form of a detailed description of her 'Land of Love'. The third frieze painting, executed by the court painter Nikolaus Prugger, is in an important position. Portraying three court ladies, it incorporates the Electress' immediate social environment in the iconographic programme. Recalling the Parcae of antiquity, the ladies, apparently knowledgable in matters of the heart, are depicted embroidering the web of destiny.

Henriette's romantic yearnings were long unfulfilled and this not least explains the late birth of the Crown Prince, Max Emmanuel. In her Heart Cabinet she immortalised her most intimate emotions, leaving us a profound insight into the thoughts and feelings of a remarkable woman.

THE PORTRAIT GALLERY AND THE PORCELAIN CABINET

The Decoration of the Portrait Gallery

The first impressive room encountered in the Residence Museum is the Portrait Gallery containing the Wittelsbach portraits (Room 4). After simply appointed antechambers, the visitor is confronted with a symphony in white and gold, setting off the subtle browns of the formal portraits. Many are overwhelmed by this Baroque exuberance and even its admirers do not immediately register the sophistication of this interior, not least the work of the wood-carver Wenzeslaus Miroffsky, until they have looked at it more closely. Joseph Effner (1687–1745), a protégé of Max Emmanuel's who trained in Paris, submitted the design in 1726. Known for his masterpieces at Schleissheim and Nymphenburg, his work in the Residence reveals him at the height of his powers. His personal idiom represents a whimsically anecdotal treatment of the most modern French interior decoration of the day. Not long afterwards, refined by François Cuvilliés, it would define the Rococo to come as the style to shape the new state apartments.

Twelve window bays mark the rhythm; the wainscot and a bold cornice define the principal architectural lines of the room. A ceiling painting, celebrating the Prince Elector Karl Albrecht, who commissioned these rooms, as the renewer of the Order of St George, emphasizes the centre of the room. Two other paintings, lost in the war, are merely indicated by touches of colour. Gilt floral, animal and implement motifs interspersed with lively sprites link the three rows of paintings.

The pair of dragons above the wainscot panels attests to the fashion in chinoiserie of the time. The fire they exhale turns into palm fronds which then develop further until becoming increasingly overgrown with lush grapevines. Heraldic animals as well as all sorts of bellicose symbols are scattered throughout with a liberal hand. The comical aspect of the tiny animal figures only becomes clear in close-up, when the sensitively captured play of their muscles in very low relief achieves an effect of great depth. The plant motifs are also delicately detailed, from minuscule leaves ruffled by a strong breeze to a stalk forming a wide arc. These motifs blend imperceptibly with the mouldings, the work of the ordering human hand that maintains the decorative system.

The delicate finishing touches were added by gilders. The subtle play of shapes is generated by a layer of chalk whiting only a millimetre thick which is the ground required for gilding with fine gold leaf. Lines engraved in this ground, surfaces, grooves, patterns and hatching create a deliberately cultivated effect of chased bronze. Subtle gold tones achieved with gold leaf only a thousandth of a hair's thickness shim-

The Wittelsbach Portrait Gallery on the ground floor of the tract named after it. Preserved as it was, François Cuvilliés' interior, which from 1730 replaced what was once an open passage, is superb by any standards.

mer from lemon yellow to orange, fiery in hue or subdued in half-tones. The ceiling stucco from the masterly hand of Johann Baptist Zimmermann finally crowns this masterpiece of a room.

The Wittelsbach Portraits

All this artistry was to promote the fame of the House of Wittelsbach and

its claim to the crown of the Holy Roman Empire. The labelling which is sometimes difficult to read and the re-arrangement of the pictures over the course of the years render a cursory inspection confusing. Nevertheless, with a bit of patience, a number of interesting points emerge.

At top centre on the main north wall is the portrait of Theodo (*d.* 511), the legendary first Duke of Bavaria. His facial features resemble those of Charles v, the Habsburg Emperor closely related to Karl Albrecht, on whose European and South American Empire the sun never set. The adjacent wall to the west boasts figures from the early and late Middle Ages linking Theodo with Charlemagne and Emperor Ludwig the Bavarian – who share central positions with Theodo in the Gallery – by entangled alliances. The paintings from Jacopo Amigoni's workshop are modelled on a cycle of monarchs by Peter Candid, which once adorned the Theatiner Corridor (Room 114). The portrait of Werner von Scheyern, clad in a fur-trimmed brocade coat, the last painting but one in the middle row, is one of the finest of this type.

East of the centre are the portraits of Karl Albrecht's immediate forebears. These are relatively complete and including their wives. As focal point in this sequence, Karl Albrecht has been moved to the central group, followed by Maria Amalia of Austria, whose portrait is one of the most expressive of all. The workshop of Georges Demarées painted these and most of the other pictures up until 1765. The series of Prince Electors of Bavaria continues along to the west on the other side of Theodo, from where the more distant ancestors have been moved to the opposite wall. Max III Joseph and Karl Theodor from the Palatinate-Sulzbach line, which inherited the succession when the old Bavarian branch became extinct in 1777, then also remained without heirs. The five kings of Bavaria from the Palatinate-Zweibrücken line reigned from 1806 until 1918, when Ludwig III was deposed. Their portraits cluster about the genealogical table on the window side.

The end walls are entirely covered with paintings and can only properly be seen when the cleverly concealed doors are closed. To the east are the portraits of the most important clerics among the Wittelsbach descendents, who, among other domains, ruled the Electorate of Cologne from 1583 to

Part of a wall in the Portrait Gallery. Wenzeslaus Miroffsky's playful gold decoration twines round austere portraits from Jacopo Amigoni's workshop.

A magnificent clock from the antechamber of the Rich Rooms. Originally separate pieces, the console and table clock are from Paris and have been in the Residence since 1769. The arresting gilded bronze Apollo as the sun god in his chariot is a reference to the court of Versailles.

1761. The facing end wall sports portraits of various members of the Bavarian royal family who, for example, ruled in Sweden from 1654 to 1718. Joseph Ferdinand, Prince Elector of Bavaria, the great hope of the dynasty, occupies the upper left-hand corner. When he died in 1699, the promised succession to the throne of Spain expired – and with him Bavaria lost its last realistic chance of engaging in the politics of the Great Powers.

The Treasure Vaults or Porcelain Cabinet

The Porcelain Cabinet (Room 5) was once the Treasury. Its appointments, after designs executed by François Cuvilliés up until 1733, afford an instructive comparison illustrating the way design has changed in the seven years since the completion of the Portrait Gallery. It has become even more whimsical, delicately linear and abstract. The precious objects displayed behind glass are multiplied by a host of mirrors to create an image of incredible opulence. This fragile cultural inheritance was given a safer home in 1897, since when it has been replaced by somewhat less spectacular porcelain pieces. The exchange has not, however, impaired the dramaturgy of this suite of rooms. Since they have been preserved largely in their original state, in their own right they are among the greatest treasures in the Residence.

THE RICH ROOMS
(REICHE ZIMMER)

The Functions of the Electoral Apartments

The best view of the Electoral suite of apartments, the heart of the Residence, is to be had from the Antler Corridor (Room 99), a light-filled, narrow passage with hunting trophies. Bavaria was ruled from these apartments for about two centuries and it was here that the Wittelsbachs loved to display their sophisticated taste and flaunt the material prosperity on which it fed.

It was also here that the Free State of Bavaria found suitable accommodation when, trying to attain a new reputation in the world, Queen Elizabeth II paid her first state visit to Germany. In order to grasp the sequence of the rooms and their overall design, their original function should be understood.

Top priority was given to diplomatic protocol. After assembling in the Fountain Court (see illus. pp. 46/47), a legation would walk into the tower building past a guard of honour. The first room they would reach is what is now the Knights of St George Hall. From there they would proceed through antechambers, to be welcomed both at each door (which were usually closed) and at the centre of each room by a colonel, Marshal to the Court, a colonel chamberlain or a colonel steward of the household. The Prince Elector would then receive his guests in the Audience Chamber. The possibilities offered by varying the number of members of the Court present, the number and intimacy of the rooms occupied and, finally, the distance the Prince Elector came to meet his guest, were numerous.

Together with the foreign guests, the nobility of the capital city was regularly invited to festive events at the Residence. The attractions included concerts and dances, card-playing evenings, cultured conversation and the opportunity for intrigue. The magnificent formal rooms were also available for this purpose, especially those in the south tract, which were festively lit so as to show off the treasures they contained.

The function of the living quarters was more variable since what was required depended on the changing circumstances in the lives of its occupants. The Prince Elector Karl Albrecht, with whom we are mainly concerned here, owned a suite of private rooms on the ground floor. After considerable alteration, they are now a showcase for eighteenth-century porcelain (see p. 129).

From 1730 the Munich court was particularly challenged by the question of prestige. After all, the Wittelsbachs had great aspirations in assuming the succession of their relations, the Habsburgs, since there was no prospect of a Habsburg male heir. The dream of the Imperial crown that had sustained Wittelsbachs hopes for centuries seemed to be in their grasp when the great fire of December 1729 gutted the state rooms which had just been remodelled by Joseph Effner. This was the time for a grand re-design. Research has attempted to differentiate between Effner's plans and the forward-looking designs submitted by François Cuvilliés, who was to dominate the field from then on. What is regarded as the main achievement of the Rich Rooms however does not lie in detail since the

The Inner Audience Room was the setting for diplomatic ceremony in the Munich Residence. The wall panelling incorporating a Four Seasons cycle sets off portraits of the earliest occupants: the Prince Elector Karl Albrecht and his wife, Maria Amalia of Austria.

same artists were still at work. More importantly, fresh creative powers achieved the *tour de force* of reconciling princely apartments, which were on a truly Imperial scale, with the special claims of Viennese and – at the same time – Versailles court ceremony. This entailed arranging the suite of rooms and appointing them in the best taste and with the greatest opulence imaginable, to match the exalted status coveted by their chief occupant.

The Diplomatic Suite

The suite begins with the former Knights or Banquet Hall, which is now known as the Knights of St George Hall (Room 54) because this was where the Wittelsbachs' own order of knights used to meet in the days of King Ludwig II. Remodelled for this purpose in the late nineteenth century, it was so altered after World War II that it could easily be overseen. François Cuvilliés' model of the palace, which is displayed here, should however not be missed. It represents a serious attempt made in 1765 at a large-scale remodelling (see illus. p. 19) but the project was never realized. This is really the only place in the Residence where the visitor can gain a clear overview of the complex – which is even more monumental now than it was then – without having to take to the air.

The so-called Effner Rooms, the Antechamber and the Outer Audience (Rooms 55 and 56) in which the moderate forms of the first Late Baroque renovation have been retained, were destroyed completely and have been reconstructed on simpler lines. The white and gold of the panelling is now dominated by the elegant red of a Genoese velvet with a large flower pattern which was recreated from original scraps. The two tiled stoves shown together in the Antechamber, which are not as in the original arrangement because only one stove was saved from each of the two rooms, lend a sculptural note to the décor.

The four console tables at the window piers are superb pieces from the court workshops. They were carved by Joachim Dietrich after designs by Cuvilliés for the Treasury. The legs of these pieces are splendidly exuberant examples of Baroque design, composed of mountain-goat horns, dolphin heads and dragons' caves with their denizens. Unfortunately, the mirrors which went with them and reached the ceiling have been lost.

Among the paintings a full-figure portrait of the Prince Elector Max Emmanuel is particularly noteworthy. It hangs on the long wall of the Antechamber with a portrait of his second wife, the Electress Therese Kunigunde of Poland. The portraits are the work of Joseph Vivien. Max Emmanuel looks particularly lifelike thanks to the subtle use of pastel. The paintings of the first twelve Roman Emperors above the doors of the Effner Rooms and the Inner Audience Room are copies after Titian.

The Inner Audience Room (Room 57), where offical state receptions were held, has retained its original appearance. The most important modern reconstruction is – and this is the case throughout the main floor – the ceiling, a perfect copy after Zimmermann.

Roelant Savery, 'Paradise'. This exuberant view of nature by a Flemish painter is representative of the large collection of Netherlandish paintings in the Green Gallery.

Individual symbolic figures relate the art of ruling the state, which is guided by Prudence, Fortune, Courage in Battle and Wisdom, to cosmic symbols associated with the Four Seasons (on the window wall) and the Four Elements (above the corners of the room). The

The main room of the Green Gallery. The largest room in the Rich Rooms, it was reached via a grand stair – no longer there – through the portals visible at the left.

carving of the wall panelling is, under Cuvilliés' influence, more subtle than that of the Portrait Gallery although the underlying concept has remained the same.

Above the entrance Peter Candid's portrait of the emperor Ludwig the Bavarian supplements the complete cycle of Roman emperors which adorns the overdoors so that here, as in the Antiquarium, antiquity is linked with the medieval Holy Roman Empire which still existed. The portraits of the last Wittelbach on the imperial throne, Karl Albrecht and his wife Maria Amalia (Joseph Vivien painted their portraits in 1722) are a convincing addition made in the course of (modern) restoration.

Incidentally, it was not the throne placed on a platform which lent regal dignity to the sovereign, who stood during the audience, it was the baldachin above him. Elaborate lighting, which was reflected many times over by almost full-length mirrors, added to the overall lustre. However, the furniture also played an important role. The

Jean-Marc Nattier, 'Tsar Peter the Great', signed and dated 1717. This state portrait of the Russian Tsar is one of the prize works in the Green Gallery.

two commodes by the master cabinet-maker Charles Cressent are notable for their sculptural design. These sumptuous luxury items with gilded bronze mounts were brought, like the mirrors, from Paris. The watches and clocks exhibited here were greatly admired and even more so the china which had to be imported from Japan as long as the making of hard-paste porcelain remained a secret in the West.

The Green Gallery (Grüne Galerie)

Cuvilliés' gallery wing was the most important new addition to the Portrait Gallery complex. Its splendidly proportioned façade can best be appreciated on the way to the Portrait Gallery. Two double-panelled doors are all that indicate the position of the original entrance to the Gallery Room, formerly also a banqueting hall, from the garden. The reconstructed wall decoration, notably the silk damask after which the Green Gallery (Room 58) has been named, represents a further development of the overall design used in the rooms of state. The paintings are hung decoratively as they were. Many of them have remained in place of the original appointments even though the most valuable paintings have been moved to the State Galleries.

Franz Snyders, a colleague of Rubens' and pupil of Pieter Brueghel the Younger, painted the still lifes on the overdoors of the lobby, which are typical examples of their genre; next to each are Dutch versions of the same. The main painting on the wall as one enters, a *Hagar with Ishmael in the Desert*, is the work of Luigi Garzi, a Roman painter. The scene of *Mary Magdalene Washing Christ's Feet* by a pupil of Tintoretto's, hung below it, is hardly inferior to it as a composition.

The most monumental works in the Green Gallery dominate the northern chimney wall. The Venetian painter Antonio Zanchi was summoned to

State bedroom in the Rich Rooms suite. The sumptuously embroidered wall hangings are particularly fine.

Munich to execute the (destroyed) altarpiece for the Theatine Church. His work is at least still with us in the paintings here of *Joseph Introducing His Brothers to Pharaoh* and *The Good Samaritan*. The Munich court painter Nikolaus Prugger is more reticent in tone. His portraits of the ageing court official Balthasar Camerlocher and his wife, which flank the chimney-breast, are among the highlights of the collection. On a level with them, in the right-hand corner of the room, is a work one might well mistake as a

Rembrandt. However, the shy *Orientale* is the work of Aert de Gelder, who makes no bones about who his teacher was.

On the wall with the mirror-panelled door, Roelant Savery, a Flemish painter active in 1600, has turned his *Paradise* into a cheerful zoology text-book. Below it, Adam Franz van der Meulen, Court Painter to Louis XIV, the Sun King, has depicted the *Battle of Dinant* in meticulous detail.

Two fine pieces dating from the reign of Duke Maximilian I grace the

The Mirror Cabinet in the Rich Rooms suite as it was in 1958. Visitors in the eighteenth-century were amazed by the illusionist effect of suites of rooms created by multiple reflections. The invention of large mirrors with flawless glass made such sophisticated whimsies possible.

arch wall. On the left is Hans von Aachen's *Bathsheba* succumbing to the blandishments of King David. Across from it hangs a *Holy Family with St John as a Boy*, a motif that recurs frequently in the collection. In it Peter Candid has made effective use of his favourite cool burgundy red.

On the long east wall is Jusepe de Ribera's *St James the Greater*, a typical representative of Baroque naturalism in the Caravaggio manner. To the side of the central mirror Carlo Maratta's heads from an *Annunciation* in light tones represent Roman High Baroque. Some time should be spent in front of the last row of pictures: Hermann Elbel's *St Cecilia* looks more like an elegant Rococo lady and this is, in fact, a portrait of a Wittelsbach from the Palatinate line. The work is influenced by the exquisite portraiture of Georges Desmarées, who was Elbel's teacher. Above it a river landscape by Ferdinand Kobell, probably one of the most recent paintings here, anticipates the accurate observation of nature so typical of nineteenth-century painting.

Looking into the light makes it difficult to see the paintings hung on the window wall yet these are fine pieces. The earliest, *Virgin with the Infant Christ and St John* (at the top, at the second column from the south) has tentatively been attributed to Francesco Granacci, a friend of Michelangelo's. There is also *Boy Playing the Bass Viol* (1707), captured by Louis Silvestre, the director of the Dresden Academy. However, pride of place in this collection goes to a superb portrait of Tsar Peter the Great of Russia, a masterpiece (1717) from the hand of Jean-Marc Nattier.

Cuvilliés Rises to a Crescendo in the Rich Rooms

The Munich type of state-room was long criticized for forcing visitors to change direction in both the Green Gallery and the Audience Chamber. However, if one stands where the axes of the rooms cross, the splendid effect of such a 'junction' can be clearly seen. The doors seem to open up an endless vista of new suites of rooms. Even after realizing that mirror-panelled fake doors are the device which creates this effect, one can well imagine how these huge, virtually flawless mirrors – a novelty in the late Baroque era – must have delighted and puzzled the people who first saw them.

The rooms that follow were once chosen to be the social focus of the Holy Roman Empire. They were at their best when the nobility was amusing itself at court in the French manner. This exalted class was known for the fastidiousness with which it exacted the utmost in wit, charm and perfect execution of interior decorators. Munich was indeed fortunate in possessing a genius like Cuvilliés to satisfy such sophisticated taste.

His brilliant idea, informing the dramatic interiors he designed, was to keep on surpassing himself by continuing towards a crescendo from room to room as the intimacy of the chambers increased. At roughly the same level as the Inner Audience Chamber is the adjacent Conference Room to the

Lacquer commode by the ébéniste Bernard II Vanrisamburgh from the State bedroom in the Rich Rooms. It came from Paris in about 1730 with other similar pieces.

Hans Bol, 'Fair', watercolour on vellum, 21.2 x 14.1 cm, marked and dated 1592. There are twenty-one works from his hand in the Cabinet of Miniatures.

west (Room 59) which was used for private audiences and, therefore, also belonged to the diplomatic suite. This juxtaposition makes the royal bedchamber (Room 60) all the more stunning. Its walls are almost entirely covered with original carvings which frame four huge mirrors. The alcove for the bed is detached from the rest of the room by a surrounding balustrade to great effect. Moreover, it is lined at the back with costly embroidered velvet hangings for which Jean François Bassecour charged more than 70,000 guilders. The furnishings, all original except for the bed, are equally opulent. They were made by Bernard II Vanrisamburgh, a celebrated Paris *ébéniste*. The elegantly curvilinear form, hugged by fluid gilded bronze mounts, is matched by rich, glossy lacquer finish and decoration. Applied in subtle tints, the lacquer painting is a skilful, albeit rather flowery, imitation of East Asian lacquer which was so highly prized at the time. Overpowered by the lavishness of such appointments, the delicately allusive allegory transmitted by the ceiling stucco and the paintings – love scenes from antiquity, the hours of

the day, and other elements of the education of courtiers – is reduced to mere ornament. This room was not used for sleeping nor was a 'lever' in the manner cultivated by the Sun King held here. This was a luxurious guest-room, where distinguished visitors were expected to be properly impressed while appreciating the tribute paid to Bavaria's ally, France.

The adjacent Mirror Cabinet (Room 61) boasts a prime example of sumptuously veneered, showy furniture – primarily conceived as sculpture – in the little secrétaire built into the wainscot to counterbalance the fireplace. In a felicitous meeting of minds, the architect as designer has here consistently worked out the close links between architecture and appointments along French lines in close collaboration with the court sculptor Guilelmus de Groff.

The *trompe-l'œil* effects created in it are the main attraction of this cabinet. Cuvilliés has succeeded brilliantly in conjuring up a fairy-tale palace in miniature, turning a small bounded space into an apparently infinite yet co-ordinated dazzle of reflected wall carvings, rare porcelain, windows, doors and the suite itself, receding in staggered planes into the distance. The secret is the slight curve in the north wall beside the alcove.

The last room in the suite is the Cabinet of Miniatures (Room 62), the most intimate point of the imperial apartments, symbolically the heart of the Empire. It is easy to understand why it took years to even think about restoring the panelling, which had been destroyed in the fire of 1944. Fortunate circumstances spared the little pictures with their frames and the door panels which are masterpieces of their kind. A deep red, inspired by East Asian lacquer, gleams from the walls to be set off by exquisitely fine and lively carving by Joachim Dietrich. It provided the guideline for the faintly raised tracery of gold on the walls glittering with a web of bizarre scenes. The incredible leap in scale separating the architecture of the palace from the 129 paintings caught up in it has thus been convincingly achieved. The best of these paintings, the work of the Flemish artist Hans Bol (1534–93), are distinguished by their creator's ambitious rendering, in the most minute detail, of sweeping landscapes teeming with people within the scope of miniatures not exceeding the size of sheets of writing-paper. Following on the fairytale palace that is the Mirror Cabinet, these miniatures represent a microcosm of the world. What we see here are only copies since the originals are undergoing restoration – something that will still take some time. Later they may be exhibited, not as part of a decoration scheme but as an attraction in their own right, where they can be admired in all their richness close up.

A door panel from the Cabinet of Miniatures. Such pieces of architectural ornament survived the fire of 1944 to become models for reconstructing the panelling in this technique.

Over 250 metres long, the Court Garden façade of the Banqueting Hall Building is Munich architecture at its most impressive. The central tract with its porch once marked the centre of power in the Kingdom of Bavaria.

Neo-Classical Architecture

The King's Building (Königsbau)

The royal Residence was finished in time for the wedding of Maximilian II, later king of Bavaria, on 12 October 1842. Finally the vast square complex was faced on all sides with façades which matched its standing as the focal point of a respectably large country.

The King's Building, with which Ludwig I launched his ambitious renovation scheme, has often been flatteringly compared with the Palazzo Pitti in Florence but the resemblance is confined mainly to the third floor, which is recessed on both sides. The articulation of the façades was also inspired by Florence – in this instance, Leon Battista Alberti's Palazzo Rucellai. The eclecticism evident in borrowings from such a blend of models is due to the Crown Prince's changing preferences. His fickleness in matters of style represented a never-ending challenge to his architect, Leo von Klenze, a stylistic purist if ever there was one.

Nevertheless, Klenze managed to create a distinctive aesthetic whole. Its salient features are a stately row of twenty-one arched windows above the forcefully weighty rustication of the ground floor, which – with the sole interruption of the middle portals – rests on a Cyclopean nailhead frieze. The clear proportions of this façade have been achieved by articulating it in five parts, of which four sections over three floors with two squares are clustered about one of the central axes. Klenze thus created a distinctive aesthetic unity of a sedate solemnity which entirely suited Ludwig's ideas of public architecture. An extension of the façade, articulated by seven axes, takes it round the west corner, where, as the 'Dowager Tract', it links up with the older parts of the complex and reveals a distinctive appearance of its own. The differences in height between the already existing opera house, the buildings to the west and south of Max-Joseph-Platz and Maximilian's Residence façade have been compensated for so successfully that the many detailed elements of the city surrounding the Residence have been counterbalanced in accordance with its medieval origins.

In order to set apart the Royal apartments from the stuccoed façades which are so typical of Munich, this section was given a front of natural stone composed of massive green ashlar blocks hewn near Kelheim. Its subtle play of colours was exploited for a number of other monumental buildings or, to save money, was imitated in painted stucco.

The Banqueting Hall Building on the Court Garden

At the latest by 1780, when the Court Garden was made accessible to the public, something had to be done about the Residence's unattractively cluttered north façade. The first king to have his private apartments here in about 1800 was content at first merely to have the rhythm of the fenestration altered. The royal apartments of state, for which the sumptuousness of late Baroque was no longer desired as it was out of date, would be built by his son. On 18 October 1832 Ludwig I laid the cornerstone and again it was Klenze who had submitted the plans for the new building.

The court architect had to plan the preservation of the Imperial Court tracts with their projecting corners in mind. A good opportunity for creating something new was at the north-west corner of the complex after the city fortifications had been demolished. This was to be a striking end pavilion, which would also be linked visually with the King's Building. Mirroring this section of the façade with a companion-piece had been a project planned around 1800 by the architect Maximil-

The façade of the King's Building as the backdrop to Max-Joseph-Platz. In 1826, a year after his coronation, King Ludwig I embarked on the building of the new wing which, together with the somewhat earlier National Theatre, powerfully demarcates the Residence from the city centre.

ian von Verschaffelt and it was readily taken up again. Verschaffelt's project also offered the ideal solution to the problem of emphasizing the central tract, which seemed the most fitting place for a new Throne Room. The major architectural challenge faced by the designer of the Banqueting Hall Building was its external appearance. The boldly projecting porch, combining arcades and columns in an exceptional way, became the dominant element of this wing, which is more than 250 metres long. It now forms the entrance to the best concert hall in the city. The sculptural ornament which was deliberately left off the King's Building returns triumphantly here. Framed by heraldic lions, symbols of the eight districts of Bavaria recall the enlargement of the country's territory

in 1806 by the incorporation of Franconia and Swabia.

The East Tracts

The harmony of the stately Court Garden façade becomes perceptibly more taut around the corner of the eastern pavilion on the approach to the headquarters of the Max Planck Society, finished in 1999. Its glass façade is tied in primarily with the Staatskanzlei, the seat of the Bavarian Prime Minister, at the lower end of the Court Garden. The central dome, concealing an unabashedly historicizing Hall of Fame which occasionally can be visited, is all that remains of the Bavarian Army Museum, built after plans by Ludwig Mellinger and finished in 1905.

By 1842 Klenze had also cleared the eastern approach to the Residence, which, since the Neuveste burnt down, had been a romantic array of patched ruins and rampant green. For some decades the court apothecary was housed here, giving the adjacent court its name. Marstall Platz, originally a wide green space, was laid out here. Not until after World War II was it blocked by a scenery depot of the Opera House so that an entire main façade of the Residence was lost to Munich.

From a north-western relic of Marstall Platz the Bavarian Academy of Sciences and Humanities is now entered. Across from it, a new building matching it in style conceals the northern end of a storage facility. It is used by the Instituto Cervantes, a Spanish cultural institution. The centre of the square is marked by a fountain commemorating Rupprecht (*d.* 1955), the last heir to the Bavarian throne.

All Saints' Court Church is squeezed into the narrow rear courtyard of the State Opera House. Its façade, like that of the King's Building, is remarkable for being articulated purely by natural stone blocks, whose delicate stonemasonry is conditioned by the central wheel window. Konrad Eberhard's relief in the tympanum of the main portal shows the Judge of the World surrounded by the symbols of the Evangelists. Flanking figures of the Apostles Peter and Paul represent the Church as an institution of spiritual power. The loss of the south side wing (it was sacrificed to the theatre buildings in 1950) and the grenade scars left as a warning against war for future generations have given Klenze's masterpiece of a church an arresting new look. The interior is currently being turned into a cultural centre.

All Saints' Court Church, finished in 1837. It dominated Marstall Platz until insensitive postwar urban planning consigned it to rear courtyard status.

The Apothecary Court (Apothekenhof)

On returning to the Crown Prince Rupprecht Court, pass through the entrance to the Apothecary Court, the largest open space contained within the complex. It echoes the form of the Banqueting Hall tract, which frames the north and east side with its austere rear façade. Renaissance tracts are concealed behind its other façades: in the south is the Charlotte Corridor, which once led to the Neuveste; in the west the Trier tract, its two-storey arcades now effectively fenestrated in the upper floor, stand out sharply against the steeply pitched roof of the Imperial Court Tracts. Between the parked cars a few lines in the paving can be seen. These trace the outline of the fortification casemates (see photo p. 10) and are all that remains above ground of the old moated castle. Guided by the dominating Residence Tower, pass through the Fountain Court and back across the Chapel Court to the city side.

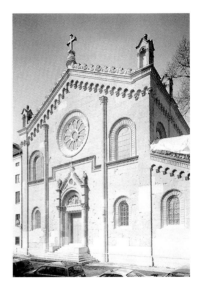

King Ludwig I was especially assertive where the King's Building was concerned. Klenze, his architect, groaned in despair at many of his royal patron's unusual notions: "It is difficult to imagine more utterly impossible architecture than in these plans." When Ludwig demanded that no wood, silk or mirrors should be used, he was breaking with a formative tradition of palace architecture. He did so because, as a patriotic German, he condemned the French origin of that style. Instead, he envisaged Italian marble floors and huge fresco cycles in the grand manner of the Palazzo del Tè in Mantua. As can be seen, the wily court architect contrived to circumvent these restrictions in the royal apartments. On the other hand, Klenze succeeded in an impressive manner in shifting the royal dreams of grandeur to the realisation of the theatrical Nibelung Halls. Even more than through the cycle of paintings, visitors are invited to appreciate Klenze's genius as a creator of interiors on a scale which has not been preserved elsewhere in Munich, where his ideas of design once reigned supreme. Klenze, whose art was informed with the aesthetic principles of ancient Greece, never ceased to condemn his predecessors. Here the differences between his and especially Cuvilliés' aesthetic are strikingly apparent.

Like their Mediterranean counterparts, the five halls in the western part of the ground floor in the King's Building sport domed ceilings, a feature which ensured their surviving the raging fires of 1944 in relatively good condition. Contrasting sharply with the simple cubic design of the earlier rooms of state, Klenze's Nibelung Halls feature alternating barrel vaults and domes to create variety and interest. Secondly, they are differently articulated. Whereas Cuvilliés devoted his considerable skills to blurring the boundaries between wall and ceiling, framing element and surface, Klenze, committed as he was to Neo-Classicism, was proud to flaunt the linear articulation of his system of proportions as a legible legacy. The same contrast informs their treatment of detail. Klenze repeated his precise acanthus leaves, papyri and rosettes like designs on a carpet. His predecessor, by contrast, had done his best to never use any form more than once. The austere eighteenth-century triad of white, gold and red yielded to a symphony of iridescent colour combinations of burgundy red, lime green and ochre. To this end, Klenze reinstated the art of simulating marble on coloured stucco as already encountered at its best in the Stone Rooms and the Reiche Kapelle. The complex mosaics of Klenze's stone floors also combined costly materials

The interior of All Saints' Church was once lavishly adorned with frescoes. Bare walls faced with closely bonded red brick are a reminder of the destructiveness of war.

The Hall of the Wedding from the Nibelung Suite. Much of Leo v. Klenze's interior decoration has survived. The photo was taken before 1944.

with sophisticated polychromy. His technique of gilding, however, was artless compared to the eighteenth century. Progressing from room to room, the colour scheme vividly traces how the golden age of the Nibelung heroes of Burgundy at the zenith of their fortunes turns into ominous reds symbolically presaging their blood-drenched doom.

Julius Schnorr von Caroldsfeld's Nibelung Frescoes

King Ludwig shared the enthusiasm felt for the *Nibelungenlied* by many more intellectual contemporaries, who, after Napoleon's defeat envisaged a new flowering of a united Germany. Written down in about 1200, this epic perhaps handed down orally from the

great migrations of the Dark Ages, was regarded to be as important as the *Odyssey*. Karl Simrock's 1827 edition of the *Nibelungenlied* reawakened interest in the heroic material which King Ludwig wanted to see celebrated as he thought it deserved to be as a fundamental work of German literature.

Peter Cornelius, the creator of the celebrated frescoes in the Glyptothek and the Pinakothek Museums, was his original choice to execute the Nibelung paintings. When that failed to work out, the king's eye fell on Julius Schnorr von Caroldsfeld (1794–1872). He, too, was a member of the Nazarene school of painting and, while still Crown Prince, Ludwig had enthused about his Ariosto Cycle in the Casino Massimo in Rome. From 1826 to 1867, Schnorr accordingly spent what amounted to the best part of his working life on the vast project in the Residence. Friedrich Olivier and Gustav Jäger were the most gifted of his many assistants.

Schnorr had to limit the work of illustrating the epic, which comprises 2,451 cantos, to essentials. He reduced the narrative to twelve central murals in the three middle halls, which are supplemented by scenes on a smaller scale on the overdoors and the vaulted ceiling. In addition, various decorative groups of figures and reliefs also carry the narrative forward.

Visitors coming from the ground floor hall of the Dowager Tract first enter the Hall of Heroes (Room 75). Here, like actors during the curtain call, they find the main protagonists of the epic. The performance starts with Kriemhild and Siegfried to the right of the entrance and Kriemhild's brother, Gunther, King of Burgundy, with his forbidding spouse Brunhilde to the left.

Tiled stove from the Hall of Heroes. Only few of these handsomely functional elements of interior design have survived.

Above them the anonymous poet is ensconced in the allegorical company of 'Märe' (epic poetry) and 'Saga' (historical tradition), on which he drew to compose his epic. To the right of the handsome tiled stove – one of the few to have survived the fire – are the protagonists of the second, tragic, strand of the narrative: Gunther's loyal vassal Hagen, accompanied by his friend Volker and his brother Dankwart.

The Hall of the Wedding (Room 76) is festively decorated with garlands of flowers. The entrance wall boasts the scene of Siegfried's return from the Saxon Wars in which the noble lowlander wooed the Burgundian Princess Kriemhild. Hagen of Tronye (with the pointed beard, in the background), hitherto the hero of the court of Worms, is now literally overshadowed by the beaming victor. Siegfried generously places the powers he won by an earlier victory over the Nibelung, who are adept in magic, at the service of his future brother-in-law. He helps Gunther to subdue the violent Brunhilde in contests of strength and thus make her his wife. The second large painting on the east wall shows Brunhilde arriving on the banks of the Rhine near Worms. The idyllic scene counterbalances the urban and martial aspect of the painting opposite. Here three women are the focal point: Ute, the Queen Mother, with her daughter Kriemhild, to whom Gunther is presenting his betrothed. The unseeing stare with which Brunhilde fixes her immediate surroundings is a sign that the initially cheerful mood has begun to cloud over. She thinks that Kriemhilde has been – at the cost of rank – married to a vassal of Gunther's, for whom she mistakes Siegfried, who is standing off to the side. The Wedding Scene on the north wall deepens the conflict between the two couples: on the one hand the happiness of the newly wed couple, on the other Brunhilde's defiant rejection of the hapless Burgundian king. Gunther's worst humiliation – his

'Hagen Slaying Siegfried', a mural by Julius Schnorr von Carolsfeld in the Hall of Betrayal. This fresco illustrating one of the key scenes of the Middle High German epic is a highlight of the cycle.

wretched wedding night – has been studiously ignored by the painter. Siegfried helped out once again by seizing Brunhilde's girdle, thus rendering her powerless. On the window wall he shows it to Kriemhild, with the naive admonition to keep this invaluable knowledge to herself.

In the next room, the Hall of Betrayal (Room 77), the conflict which has been brewing breaks out: again on the window pier we see the episode of the Queens' dispute before the church door, which was sparked off by the question of precedence. To prove that she knows who really has power, Kriemhild points to her girdle, thus deeply wounding Brunhilde's pride. Siegfried's opponent, Hagen, is only too glad to oblige his lady by avenging her shame. The most clearly composed and finest work in the cycle reveals him in the act of hurling his lance to kill the young hero. Overwhelmed with anguish, Kriemhild writhes in pain on finding the murdered man, whose corpse has been thrown before

her door. The wall at the exit finally shows the perpetrator of the dastardly deed exposed: when Hagen approaches Siegfried's corpse – lying arrayed in state in Worms Cathedral – fresh blood oozes out of the wound. Kriemhild now has the proof she needs. At the base of the vaulting, the Nibelung are shown rummaging around in their enormous treasures, which Schnorr has deliberately placed at the centre of the cycle as the ultimate symbol of power. Kriemhild is not to lose the gold and gems which were given to her by her husband on the day after their marriage: above the exit, Hagen, who has stolen the treasure, is shown sinking it in the Rhine.

In going on to the Hall of Vengeance (Room 78), we make a leap in time which takes us to the second, originally separate, section of the *Nibelungenlied*. After a protracted widowhood, Kriemhild has married Etzel, the rich king of the Huns, who has given her the wherewithal to seek the vengeance she has plotted. Her invitation has lured distant relations to the middle reaches of the Danube. Their eventful journey is only hinted at in a handful of scenes. In the first monumental painting encountered on the window wall, Hagen is shown taking up the gauntlet on his arrival at Etzel's court: with Siegfried's magic sword on his knees, he refuses to pay homage to Kriemhild as Queen of the Huns. The last chance of reconciliation has been irrevocably lost.

Antonio Canova: 'Venus Italica', white marble, 1804–11. Crown Prince Ludwig acquired this nude sculpture, inspired by the Florentine Venus Medici and now in the lobby of the Yellow Stair to the collection.

It does not really matter in this summary how the murderous plot unfolds in a series of scheming devices, violent and vengeful deeds and repeated massacres. The main picture on the west wall summarizes all this action at its culmination: under Hagen's leadership the Burgundians are depicted dashing out of Etzel's burning palace to mow down the Huns, who greatly outnumber them. It is left to Dietrich of Berne (Verona), who is Theoderic, a borrowing from another saga, to put an end to the slaughter. At Kriemhild's behest he has finally managed to beat Hagen, who was his friend, to the ground, as we see in the central field of the north wall. The privilege of beheading Hagen is reserved for Kriemhild in the last painting. Although the revenge is wrought by Dietrich's old comrade Hildebrand, her life is also forfeit.

As in the Hall of Heroes, the Hall of Complaint (Room 79) finishes off this bleak main strand of the narrative. Among a train of mourners, two Bavarian kings make their appearance: Ludwig I, who commissioned the epic cycle, and his grandson, Ludwig II, who brought it to completion. The elder, crowned with a laurel wreath, can also be seen as can his youthful companion, at the side of Queen Ute, who has broken down.

The aesthetic quality of Julius Schnorr von Carolsfeld's frescoes was questioned from the outset. It is true that he did not recapture the brilliant palette which had made his early work so famous in Rome. Some carelessness has also crept into his handling of figure modelling and this defect has been magnified in restoration. Having lost the other Residence fresco cycles – among them, notably, Schnorr's three Imperial Halls and the six Odyssey Halls with paintings by Johann Georg Hiltensperger in the Banqueting Hall Building as well as the frescoes in All Saints' by Heinrich von Hess – we are grateful to possess this probably grandest of all nineteenth-century fresco cy-

Peter von Hess: The Encounter at Wörgl', oil on canvas, 1832/33. The painting belongs to a cycle of fourteen battle pieces from the Napoleonic wars.

cles left to Bavaria. In scope and sweep it is worthy of Richard Wagner's epic musical treatment of the theme.

THE ROYAL APARTMENTS

The King's Private Chambers

The suite of rooms on the main floor of the King's Building has been restored, in the main, to as it was in King Ludwig's day; the overall concept has been recaptured but its aesthetic unity is impaired. The planners responsible for reconstruction first had to forgo Leo von Klenze's details in order to recreate the whole in the style of the new Treasury. Still the Battle Halls (Rooms 14a–14c) are worth a visit, if for no other reason to recall the Banqueting Hall Building as it was before it was gutted. Its most important panel paintings, to which the eastern end pavilion was devoted, have found a new home here.

The cycle of history paintings commissioned by Duke Maximilian I, the Schleissheim battle pieces owned by the Prince Elector Max Emmanuel and

his own feeling towards the period of change inspired Crown Prince Ludwig to order some similarly documentary works. While still Colonel-General in Napoleon's army, he commissioned Wilhelm von Kobell, a talented landscape painter, to embark on the first pieces in the battle cycle. Kobell's scenes of the siege of Breslau and the victorious campaigns against Austria from Arnhofen to Wagram are shown in the Second Battle Hall (Room 14b). Here one of the finest works in the series has been hung; it is typical of this painter's innocent delight in detail: Peter von Hess's *Encounter at Wörgl* (1809). A Bavarian unit, recognisable by their 'caterpillar helmets', attacks a handful of Tyrolese partisans against a dramatic Alpine background.

Joseph Stieler's well-known portrait of King Ludwig I in coronation regalia adorns the window pier (see illus. p. 22); it makes the man who built the Neo-Classical Residence come to life as both a statesman and patron of the arts.

Immediately adjacent to the Third Battle Hall, with six paintings depicting the downfall of Napoleon's '*Grande Armée*', is the King's Throne Room

The King's Throne Room represented the highpoint of court ceremony and design in the King's Apartments. The motifs of the wall reliefs, taken from Pindar's Odes, were designed by Ludwig Schwanthaler.

An old colour photo of the King's Service Room (now the Third Battle Hall) shows its original decoration in the Pompeiian manner. This room and the king's other antechambers were redesigned in a moderate Neo-Classical style.

(Room 127). This, the largest room in the suite, reveals Klenze's formal idiom unchanged. The decoration is all in white and gold. Intended for use as a semi-private audience chamber, it now stands for what was once the focus of royal Bavarian court ceremony since the great Throne Room has been lost. Like the entire suite, it is informed with the Neo-Classical response to ancient Greek poetry. After the myth of the Argonauts, the epics of Hesiod and Homer, Pindar, the Classical lyric poet of sports on an elegant plane, sets the tone in the iconographic programme. Ludwig Schwanthaler, creator of the monumental statue of *Bavaria*, and one of the most prolific masters represented in the King's Building, translated it into stucco reliefs. Nearly three hundred figures from the 'Odes' are captured in famous ancient sports contests. Dwarfed by these reliefs, the furniture, except for the throne, which

was retrieved from Banqueting Hall Building to replace the lost original. Its gold embroidery on red velvet attests to the continuing high standards of craftsmanship at the court workshops.

The king's private apartments which follow reveal Klenze at his best in inventive interior decoration. The Queen's Apartments, however, are better preserved.

The Queen's Apartments

These are reached via the marble spiral of the Queen Mother's Stair (Room 72), which has been cleverly tucked into the wedge-shaped plan of the Dowager Tract. As in the Gate Hall entering from Max-Joseph-Platz, Klenze's original interior decoration has remained intact. On reaching the queen's rather bare antechambers the visitor is confronted with a strikingly restored

An encaustic painting with a scene from Gottfried August Bürger's 'Song of a Valiant Man', executed by Philipp Foltz in an ancient technique revived to refurbish the Queen's Service Room.

gem typical of the Royal Apartments: a parquetry floor of sycamore, ebony and mahogany which is notable for the fineness of the designs on it. The architect was successful in talking his royal patron out of a cold stone floor by pointing out that, with parquetry, he could achieve colour effects similar to those known from Pompeiian houses. The craftsmanship of antiquity also inspired the decoration of the walls. After a protracted period of experimentation, the encaustic technique of painting with pigments mixed with molten beeswax was revived. The best place to admire the rich matt finish achieved with encaustic is the Queen's Service Room (Room 117), where the employees closest to her worked. Klenze suggested scenes from German poetry as its theme to add a contemporary touch to offset the classical canon informing the king's apartments. Following on the medieval courtly poets Walther von der Vogelweide and Wolfram von Eschenbach, work by Gottfried August Bürger, a contemporary of Goethe's, was drawn on for the Service Room. His 'Song of a Valiant Man' has retained much of its original quality.

Even though the adjacent Queen's Throne Room (Room 118) impresses some visitors as bold and eye-catching, most succumb in spite of themselves to the sheer magnificence of its gold walls.

The next room, a saloon or sitting-room (Room 119) contains the most opulent parquetry floor of its type. The green tints of the wall decoration pale next to it. Klenze had created a prime example of Roman-inspired decoration modelled on what he had studied in Pompeii in 1832. Although the frieze running round the room now looks rather sketchy, you can still pick out scenes from Christoph Martin Wieland's pseudo-medieval verse-tale 'Oberon'. Here most of the colour surfaces are original and can be better understood as a general historical message than exact restoration would have permitted.

The furnishings of this sitting-room, which opened into the royal private apartments to the north, are also remarkable. Consisting of wall consoles, a round centre table and extensive seating, they were – like most of the original furnishings left in the King's Building – designed by Klenze and made in a Bavarian workshop. The entire gilding, the carved ornament, which is in delicate low relief on surfaces and powerful high relief on the chair arm terminals, as well as its beauty of line distinguishing the overall design go some way to explain why this suite on the whole is so effective. Other pieces, such as the writing-cabinet inlaid with intarsia from the queen's private apartments, which was in the first antechamber of this suite, are much grander yet they look lost against these bare walls. It takes the interplay of furnishings and an interior decoration scheme designed by one artist capable of imaginative design to

Chair, designed in 1834 by Leo von Klenze, for the antechambers of the King and Queen (now Room 115), walnut, with cowhide upholstery.

make one realize just how successfully the nineteenth century was still dealing with the idea of rooms as total works of art. Although so much has been lost, the apartments Klenze designed for Ludwig I are a fitting finale to any tour of the restored Residence.

The Queen's Sitting-Room. The guilt furniture and the Pompeii-inspired wall decoration were designed by Leo von Klenze. The fine parquetry floor, reconstructed by 1980, contributes substantially to the elegance of this room, whose character suffered relatively little damage.

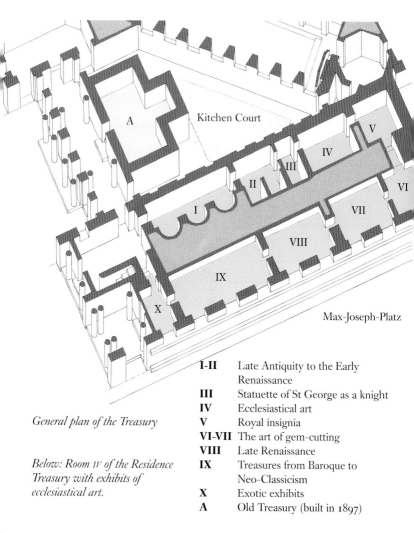

Kitchen Court

Max-Joseph-Platz

General plan of the Treasury

Below: Room IV of the Residence Treasury with exhibits of ecclesiastical art.

I-II	Late Antiquity to the Early Renaissance
III	Statuette of St George as a knight
IV	Ecclesiastical art
V	Royal insignia
VI-VII	The art of gem-cutting
VIII	Late Renaissance
IX	Treasures from Baroque to Neo-Classicism
X	Exotic exhibits
A	Old Treasury (built in 1897)

THE COLLECTIONS IN THE RESIDENCE

The Treasury (Schatzkammer)

The History of the Collection

In a document dated 19 March 1565, Duke Albrecht V declared seventeen treasures (and later ten further objects) to be unalienable possessions of the House of Wittelsbach. That date marks the founding of what is now the Residence Treasury. From that nucleus of the collection, the Duke's crystal shrine (321) and the double eagle set with diamonds owned by his wife (49) have come down to us. The Duke's passion for collecting, prudently supervised by the Humanist Hans Jakob Fugger, soon filled the Kunstkammer, the Court Library and the Antiquarium (see p. 34). Each piece added elicited the vehement protests of miserly councillors who could not foresee how Albrecht's amassing such collections would permanently enhance the reputation of his country, which was poor at the time. Provisions made then, such as ensuring that the treasure would stay in the first royal palace, are still valid to this day. The Duke's successor, Wilhelm V, contributed comparatively few pieces but they are particularly prized ones, such as the popular statuette of the Wittelsbach patron saint, St George (58).

The Prince Elector Maximilian I, who inherited his grandfather's collecting mania, saw to it that the collection was enlarged to encompass seventy-one pieces of which at least twenty-eight are still traceable today. In order to establish his 'Chamber Gallery', a combination of fine paintings and valuable art objects in his private apartments, Maximilian I transferred some treasures from the collection beginning in 1607. He also added various pieces from the Residence Kunstkammer, which was being dismantled. In 1632 Swedish troops occupied and looted

the Residence, taking jewels with them which are still highlights of Scandinavian museums. However, various legacies had swelled the Residence collections to about 600 pieces by the time Max III Joseph, the last Wittelbach of the Old Bavarian line died in 1777.

Now the collection began to grow in leaps and bounds. Although the Mann-

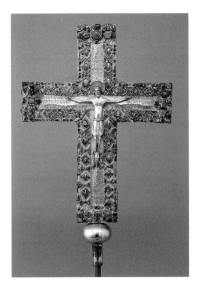

Cross of Queen Gisela of Hungary, (no. 8), made in Regensburg c. 1006. Set with pearls and precious stones, this devotional object was made for the tomb of Gisela, Duchess of Bavaria, her mother.

heim heir, the Prince Elector Karl Theodor, was forced to use some of them to pay outstanding debts, the treasures he brought with him from the Palatinate far more than compensated for what was lost. This treasure's history is as tangled as the Rhenish genealogy of this line of the Wittelsbachs, which has branches from Neuburg,

Heidelberg and Düsseldorf extending as far away as England, Sweden and Poland. Among the finest pieces are a Late Gothic crown (16) and what is known as the Holbein Bowl (40) from the English royal collections, a cup from Mannheim carved out of heliotrope, a semiprecious stone (459), and, of course, the Radziwill Bowl (592). The most important work of sculpture from the Palatinate collection is probably an ivory crucifix carved by Georg Petel of Neuburg (157). A bronze cast from Petel's model, the *Neptune* (*c.* 1630) from the Great Residence garden, which is now the King's Building Court, stands at the Broad Stair (Room 43) of the Museum rooms attesting to the versatility of this sculptor, who died young.

Not long after 1800, the turmoil of the French Revolution led in Bavaria to the confiscation of Church possessions, which had a disastrous effect on the preservation of the Bavarian heritage. Some of the most venerable of these objects have remained in the Residence Treasury: a crown dating from the early eleventh century, which was venerated in Bamberg as a relic of the Empress Kunigunde (10), and the Cross of Gisela of Regensburg (8), which is roughly contemporary.

The treasures survived the fall of the Bavarian monarchy in 1918 and the even more devastating period of World War II undamaged. Even after the Treasury was opened again to the public in 1958 acquisitions continued. A dressing-case which belonged to the last queen of Bavaria, Marie Therese, owned by the French empress Marie Louise, was acquired in 1959 by the Free State of Bavaria (939–1061).

Where the Treasures were Kept

The treasure is thought to have first been kept in the Silver Tower of the Neuveste, which rose to the northeast of what is now the Apothecary Court. When the Residence was rebuilt, a vaulted cellar was exposed to view which lends support to this conjecture. After the Silver Tower was demolished in 1612, the treasure was transferred to Duke Maximilian's private apartments above what is now the Portrait Gallery and stayed there for three generations.

The ambitious building projects launched by the Prince Elector Karl Albrecht made it necessary to move it again. On the ground floor of his living quarters, in addition to the Portrait Gallery, the Treasury formed an impressive suite attesting to Wittelsbach imperial ambitions. After a fire, which, however, spared the treasures, François Cuvilliés finished the new Treasury in 1733. Even though the vast number of pieces acquired from the Palatinate could only be piled up here, this Late Baroque treasure chamber was in use until the close of the nineteenth century. The last major building project but one in the Residence was commis-

Double eagle of Duchess Anna of Austria (no. 49), Vienna or Italy, c. 1550. Set with diamonds, this pendant was added to the treasure when the vaults were established by the wife of Duke Albrecht V, a daughter of the Emperor Ferdinand I.

The Porcelain Cabinet adjacent to the Portrait Gallery. François Cuvilliés designed it to meet the royal need for an appropriately regal setting. The Wittelsbach valuables were exhibited in the former 'Treasure vaults' from 1733 until about 1900.

sioned by Luitpold, the Prince Regent. By 1897 Julius Hofmann had built the Old Treasury, which survived, converted into an air-raid shelter in World War II.

This vaulted room was also too small for the number of exhibits. Therefore, rebuilding the Residence afforded a good opportunity of moving the treasures once more, this time to a spacious new home on the ground floor in the eastern part of the King's Building, where the court kitchens and a suite of administrative offices had once been housed. Finished in 1958, this handsome exhibition space is conservative in design. It is among the major achievements of what has been the most recent phase of construction in the Residence.

Earlier Treasures, Religious Art and the Royal Insignia

Room I is, chronologically speaking, the place to start. It boasts some examples of ancient engraved stones and important works of early medieval art. Many of these pieces once belonged to the Church, including the Prayer Book that belonged to the Emperor Charles the Bald (4), which may be the earliest extant breviary for private devotions, and King Arnulf's ciborium (5) – late ninth-century architecture in minature, decorated with gold reliefs, which contained the Eucharist. The cross owned by Queen Gisela of Hungary (8) and a cross reliquary (9) together represent the cultural flowering of the Bavarian Saxon Emperor, Heinrich II, about

1000 AD. An engraved onyx (11) from the thirteenth century is notable for being the largest known eagle cameo of the Staufen period. A collection of early crowns includes a superb north-western European work, a wreath of gold lilies set with precious stones, which may have been given by King Richard II of England to his unfortunate wife, Anne of Bohemia. Through their daughter Blanca, who married a Wittelsbach of the Palatinate line, the diadem finally passed into the possession of the Bavarian Wittelsbachs (16).

In Room II, which is devoted to the fifteenth and sixteenth centuries, the influence of sacred art still makes itself felt. A Burgundian portrait medallion (19) and a rosary, which is probably French (21), are exhibited with German, Flemish and Italian work. As it moved north of the Alps, the Renaissance was accompanied for quite some time by relics of Gothic art like some bizarre miniature carved, nut-like prayer-beads (c. 1500), which open up (28). A cup from Strasbourg, at least three decades later, is decorated with the impressions of late Roman coins (38), attesting to a well developed cult of antiquity and ancient art. The silver *Rappoltstein Cup* (43), an almost overly ornate work, celebrates the rich veins of ore found in a stretch of land in Alsace under Palatinate rule.

Duke Albrecht's chain, worn with his robes of office, is sumptuously set with precious stones (57). Together with the most popular piece in the collection, the delicate reliquary of St George, the saintly knight (58), it has been on display since 1958 in a space of its own, Room III. This piece is much more than simply a masterpiece of gem-cutting, enamelling on curved surfaces and the most sophisticated

The crown of an English queen (no. 16), Western European, c. 1370–80. This superb piece may have been owned by the Plantagenet king Richard II.

Statuette of St George as a knight (no. 58). The emblem of the Treasury, it dates from c. 1597 but its plinth was made towards 1640 to house a relic of the saint which the Archbishop of Cologne had donated. The visor conceals a portrait of his brother, Duke Wilhelm V.

Crucifix of ivory on wood stained black (no. 157), Augsburg, c. 1630. Georg Petel, who made it, was regarded as the best German sculptor of his day. He also made the monumental Neptune in the lobby of the Broad Stair in the Residence.

formed, and the crown jewels of the nineteenth century. Taken together, the St George and the chain impressively represent the spiritual and temporal power of a great European dynasty.

Later sacred art is collected in Room IV, where it is exhibited separately from the vestment collection (see p. 106) and some of the reliquaries, which have been displayed in a room of their own since 1939 (see p. 108). There is a great deal to see so let us concentrate here on a portable altar used by Duke Wilhelm V for his private devotions (60), a delicate ebony case boasting superb gold mounts (*c.* 1578) by Abraham Lotter the Elder and Ulrich Eberl of Augsburg. At the centre of the room is a somewhat earlier portable altar by the same master craftsmen (59). Unfortunately, it has lost its central pietà or *Lamentation*. The Georg Petel crucifix has already been mentioned; other superb early seventeenth-century ivory carvings are from the hand of Christoph Angermair. Notable for a subtle use of planes to suggest spatial depth, his *Crucifixion* (156) is as lavishly detailed as his carved coin shrine, which is kept in the Bavarian National Museum.

Even though the insignia of temporal power are not always the greatest works of art in a collection of treasures, they do possess a mystique of their own. This is just as true of Room V concluding the north wing of the Munich Treasury, which is devoted to the crowns of the kings and queens of Bavaria and such other symbolic objects as the Orb of Empire, the sceptre, the sword of the kingdom and a seal coffer (245–251).

Unlike the early establishment of an own state the Bavarian title of king, which was occasionally claimed retroactively in the early Middle Ages, is of much more recent origin. It dated from 1806, Bavaria's reward for remaining loyal to the alliance with Napoleon. This is also reflected

craftsmanship in gold. The face of the little equestrian is (under the visor) a portrait of the man who was its donor, Duke Wilhelm and is aesthetically convincing, apart from the opulence of its execution, as a work of Mannerist sculpture after a design by Friedrich Sustris. These last two works represent, temporally and spatially speaking, milestones midway between the era of the Emperor Heinrich the Holy, when the nucleus of the early collection was chronologically in the pieces exhibited. There was never a formal coronation during the nineteenth century. The reason for this may have been that as a Protestant, Karoline, the first queen, was not admitted to a church coronation, and that, as a result, Ludwig I hated the French Emperor, being instrumental in the establishment of the crown. After three generations of important kings, who are scarcely known beyond the borders of Bavaria, Ludwig II, the 'Fairy-Tale Monarch', ensured that the Kingdom of Bavaria would continue to figure prominently on the itineraries of latter-day fans from across the world. His tragedy consisted in his

a mystery that has never been solved.

Some memorable pieces in gold created by the French court jeweller Martin-Guillaume Biennais remain from his era and that of six other kings. What more appropriate summation of a royal Bavaria could one ask for?

The Franconian Ducal Sword (232) is notable for being a relic of what was once an independent state in today's northern Bavaria. The decorations worn by royal and aristocratic members of the Bavarian and Palatinate courts are a reminder of nobility's former social dominance. One of their patrons, the venerable Order of St George, is still flourishing in Bavaria.

The Bavarian crown and insignia of the crown including the Orb of the Kingdom and the sceptre (nos. 245–248). They were made in 1806/7 in the atelier of Martin-Guillaume Biennais, who was court jeweller to the Emperor Napoleon.

failure to reconcile his exaggerated notions of Late Absolutist monarchy with the realities of Bismarck's utilitarian German Empire. As a consequence Ludwig II withdrew from the world and found his death in Lake Starnberg,

So is the Order of the Golden Fleece, to which the Bavarian rulers generally belonged, which represents the most lofty assemblage of nobility from across Europe, transcending the bounds of Bavaria.

Kunstkammer, Later Treasures and Exotic Crafts

The next two rooms, VI and VII, have been arranged on the lines of a sixteenth-century *Kunstkammer*, that is, according to the materials of which the exhibits are made. The first room boasts creations of rock crystal and smoky quartz. The Alps were once a rich source of these minerals. Because of their unique transparency and their working which required a high degree of precision, objects made of these minerals were among the most coveted Kunstkammer pieces. An exhibit of objects made of opaque materials like agate, heliotrope and jasper follows. With their enamelled gold settings and brilliantly coloured stones, these collector's items exemplify the playful Mannerist treatment of form at its most sinuously sumptuous. At least three of these pieces deserve a closer look: first, the crystal shrine owned by Duke Albrecht V (321), an ambitious work dating from the beginnings of the collection on which Milanese and Augsburg master craftsman collaborated. Thirty-seven panels of rock crystal with Old Testament scenes incised in hollow relief are mounted on an ebony chest with architectural elements in crystal. A monumental 'Prunkvase' (328) exacted even more of the craftsmen who executed it, the Sarachi brothers of Milan, to whom the Treasury is indebted for several other masterpieces. The imposing body of the vase was carved from a single piece of crystal, polished and decorated with scenes in delicate relief. Finally, there is a superb piece of royal furniture dating from the reign of the Prince Elector Maximilian I. This highly decorated table (519) boasts a top inlaid with chased metals as well as pietra-dura work by the Prague court workshop of Cosimo Castrucci (active there 1596–1610).

'The Creation of the World', the main work in a series of engravings from the crystal shrine of Duke Albrecht V, made by Annibale Fontana of Milan in 1560/70 and set in ebony by Augsburg chest-makers and goldsmiths.

Rooms VIII and IX represent a return to the chronological ordering of the overall plan. Here pieces dating from the Late Renaissance to Neo-Classicism are displayed. The great voyages of exploration and far-flung trade links furnished craftsmen with such exotic materials as narwhal ivory (563), rhinoceros horn (1173) and even (often fake) concretions found in certain animals' digestive tracts. Known as bezoar and believed to be antidotal, they were set as elegantly as jewels. The classic art of the goldsmith, at its acme in the sixteenth century, is also represented in the Treasury by important pieces. Nuremberg was the earliest dominant centre of this craft; here one should mention the great Wenzel Jamnitzer (1508–85) who is represented by a tectonically designed jewel casket (565). Later Munich goldsmiths' workshops also attained a high standard under court patronage. A distinguished Munich goldsmith, Hans Reimer (active from 1555, d. 1604), was the maker of a standing cup (562) with a deep lobed lip. One of the finest pieces in the collection, it is set with huge sapphires and is exquisitely enamelled to flaunt the Bavarian national colours. Augsburg gradually replaced Nuremberg as the chief goldsmithing centre. A leading exponent of the craft there in Maximilian's reign was Mathias Wallbaum (1554–1632), the maker of an intricate drinking vessel in the form of a Diana group (588).

By the mid-seventeenth century, after the death of the Prince-Elector Maximilian I, the Munich Treasury had assumed the form it would continue to

Gold standing cup, decorated in white enamel and set with 36 large blue sapphires (no. 562), the Bavarian national colours. The cup was probably made after designs by the court painter Hans Mielich; it is attributed to the Munich goldsmith Hans Reimer.

Pendant of Baroque pearls and diamonds, set in silver-gilt (no. 1144), probably made in 1710/20 in Germany. From the Baroque period, curiosities as collector's items are increasingly supplanted by jewellery and objects for daily use made of precious materials.

Coffee-pot and water jug from the travelling service owned by the Empress Marie-Louise of France (Nos. 940, 941), silver-gilt, from the atelier of Martin-Guillaume Biennais, Paris 1810. The 122-piece collection of elegant objects in the Empire style for everyday use came from the estate of the last queen of Bavaria.

have. Pieces made for the Bavarian monarchs' personal use tended to be increasingly costly. Today they are also considered part of the treasure. Among these is a twenty-three-piece breakfast service with sumptuous enamel decoration (752f), which documents the acme of Augsburg craftsmanship. Finally, the most recently acquired treasure – and, at the same time, one of

the most imposing exhibits – is a model of Trajan's Column (1221) acquired by the Prince Elector Karl Theodor in 1783 in Rome, where the original rises majestically above the emperors' Forum. Its gilt relief frieze on a lapis lazuli blue ground, exemplifying the revived interest in Greco-Roman antiquity prevailing at the time, represents, in several respects, a link with the beginnings of the collection.

The exhibition finishes with exotic pieces of work which were still displayed in Late Renaissance Kunstkammer and curiosities cabinets with naive enthusiasm as equal in value with freaks of nature. Since 1958 these objects have been exhibited separately in Room x, a policy which does justice to the rarity of such pieces in the Munich collection. It is now possible to study them in the context of cultural history. In addition, these often simple yet extraordinarily rare pieces – including little Chinese porcelain bowls with per-

Putti with a sea monster. Detail of a rhinoceros-horn standing cup (no. 1173), South German showing Netherlandish influence, c. 1660. The piece is typical of early Kunstkammer objects, which were prized for the quality of the exotic materials of which they were made.

forations and dating from 1600 (1248) and a somewhat earlier carpet with hunting scenes (1240) in a superb state of preservation – thus have enough space and suitable lighting to be appreciated as they deserve. Other Persian carpets are in the East Asian Collection (see p. 123).

Even this tiny selection of works discussed here, amounting to only about three per cent of the exhibits on display, indicates that the Treasury confronts visitors with quite a challenge. A vague impression of great wealth spent with a lavish hand is often all that remains in one's memory from a quick look. This was, by the way, an effect deliberately created to further diplomacy from an apparent position of strength. Despite the limited scope available here for studying the history of the objects, which is usually quite exciting, and what they express aesthetically, the following exception will be made. The last Buddhist king of Ceylon, Bhuvaneka Bahu (reigned 1521–51), was unable to come to an amicable agreement with his brother Majadunn on the succession. Finally the king sent a life-size gold statue of his three-year-old grandson Dhamapala to his overlord, King John III of Portugal, who expressed his decision in Bhuvaneka's favour by crowning the statue. The ivory casket (1241) displayed in Room X, probably a diplomatic gift from the Singhalese, narrates this story, which is a true one, in exquisitely detailed relief. An art agent brought this little casket to Duke Albrecht's court, where it was later put into his Kunstkammer, and ultimately landed in the Treasury via the Prince Elector Maximilian's personal collection of rare artefacts. For those interested in how the Viceroy Majadunn felt about the judgement, take a look at the ivory casket no. 1242.

Coffer with domed lid, panelled with ivory reliefs and mounted with precious stones set in gold (no. 1241), once owned by a Sinhalese king. The work was acquired by Duke Albrecht V in Lisbon and is recorded from 1598 in the Munich Kunstkammer inventories.

Interior of the Sacred Vestment Rooms. These vaulted rooms on the ground floor were built in about 1600 to store the court plate silver. Since 1958 a selection of ecclesiastical vestments and altar cloths used at the Munich court have been exhibited here.

The Vestments (Paramentenkammern)

The rare German term 'Paramente' embraces liturgical vessels and altar cloths as well as the vestments worn by clergy officiating at Roman Catholic divine service, in short, anything which helps to 'prepare' (Latin 'parare') it in the appropriate manner. A legacy of late antiquity, ecclesiastical art developed particularly sumptuous forms, which have survived to the present day. Such works are interesting both from the religious standpoint and as witnesses to sophisticated and exacting crafts. Almost all luxury textiles worn and used at palaces have been lost, a further reason why the materials used by the Church, which were usually of as high quality as wall hangings and furniture upholstery in the loftiest of profane settings, can increase and

deepen our knowledge of the court life that has vanished.

There are several reasons why this area, the domain of Church museums, should be so well represented in the Munich Residence. Firstly, Duke Maximilian I was deeply religious and was anxious to have his court churches as richly appointed as possible. Quite a few textiles here, which were procured in 1615 for the Rich Chapel (see p. 49), a pet project, were so rarely used and cared for in such a strictly regulated manner that they have been preserved. Secondly, when the Prince Elector Karl Theodor caused a court bishop's see to be established in 1789, its first bishop, Joseph Ferdinand, Count Spaur, had to be fittingly invested with the external symbols of his office. Finally, the most important acquisition of rich materials and sumptuous pieces of 18th-century embroidery followed on secularization, when the possessions of great Church foundations were acquired by the court from the state mint. All Saints' Church (see p. 83), prepared magazines to receive vestments and liturgical artefacts which helped to preserve these treasures. The new building in the Romantic style also needed suitable vestments and they have survived.

The History and Focus of the Exhibition

The old Residence Museum did not have separate exhibition space to display vestments. The exhibits now on display in the new rooms were selected after reconstruction of the Museum. Three rooms on the ground floor of the Court Chapel Complex, built in about 1600 for the ducal Silver Vaults (see general plan p. 42) were made available. The well-preserved (and partly reconstructed) forms of the Late Renaissance period style, integrating ancient sculpture and that of the 16th

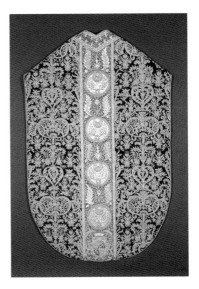

Chasuble with gold embroidery, partly in Turkey work, on dark red silk velvet. The outer garment worn by a priest celebrating mass on feast days, it was made in Munich c. 1615 and – with accessories – belonged to the appointments of the Rich Chapel.

Antependium with pattern on figured green velvet brocade. A cloth to hang over the front of the altar in the Rich Chapel, it was probably made in Italy in the early seventeenth century.

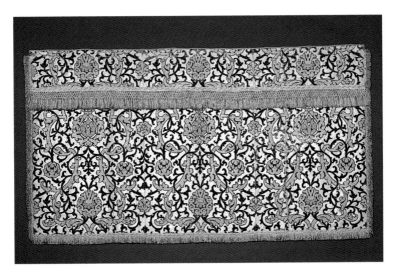

century, make a highly appropriate setting for the earlier vestments, which are outstanding. Since an exhibition entitled 'Treasures of the Church from Bavarian Palaces', mounted in Munich in 1984, occasioned thorough study of this vast collection, it has become clear how few pieces in it can be exhibited at once. It will take some time for conservation measures to be taken and adequate space to be made available for the bulk of the collection.

The First and Second Sacred Vestments Rooms (Rooms 91 and 92) are mainly devoted to acquisitions made by Duke Maximilian I for the Rich Chapel. Great quantities of gold embroidered cloth were bought in Italy between 1610 and 1615 and made by the court workshops into about 26 sets of sumptuous vestments used on feast days. Most of the everyday vestments – and no one knows how many of these there were – have been lost. The complete sets of ornate vestments and liturgical appointments included antependia (curtain-like altar cloths for the fronts of the High altar and the two side altars), a chasuble with stole and maniple (the garment used at mass which is 2/3 length and boasts strips of emblems of office round the officiating cleric's arm and torso) and covers for the missal and chalice. The occasion and importance of the Church service at which they were used are indicated by colour. The most ornate vestments for the most important feast days are in white and gold. Red was worn to symbolize veneration of the Holy Spirit, at Whitsun, for instance, or services held to commemorate particular martyrs. Feast days consecrated to the Virgin emphasized blues. Lavender indicates penitence and fasting while black vestments were reserved for funeral services. The two bishops' mitres exhibited here came to Munich from the see of Mainz. Their prized fine pearl embroidery allows a comparison of seventeenth and eighteenth-century styles, each represented by one mitre.

The Third Sacred Vestments Room (Room 93) exhibits important examples of textiles worked at eighteenth-century Upper Bavarian nunneries. A particularly important exhibit is the Wessobrunn set of vestments, donated by Empress Maria Amalia, the widow of Bavarian Charles VII, in 1749. Silver and chenille embroidery on cream-coloured satin make these vestments 'the finest example of ecclesiastical embroidery owned by the Bavarian Administration of Palaces and a superb achievement of eighteenth-century South German textiles.' (L. Seelig). Here and on the pieces comprising what is known as the Polling Vestments you can study Baroque exuberance at its most stunning as it was flaunted at important Church feast days. The abbot or bishop celebrating mass wore the mitre and was further distinguished from the other clerics officiating, who wore chasubles, by wearing the wheel-shaped cloak known as a pluvial. What is known as Dalmatics were worn by assisting deacons. The ceremonial splendour on the grand scale of High Mass, which lent the vestments their spiritual content, cannot be reproduced in a museum setting. A demonstration of ancient Bavarian piety can still be experienced today, on Corpus Christi day in June, when the famous Munich Fronleichnam procession – recorded since 1343 – passes the Residence.

The Reliquary (Reliquienkammer)

The History of the Collection and its Importance

The Residence Museum Reliquary (Room 95) is provocative to say the least. Who would not be upset by being directly confronted with the bones of saints encased in gold or children's mummies encrusted with jewels? Yet well into the eighteenth century, this cabinet of spiritual wonders was re-

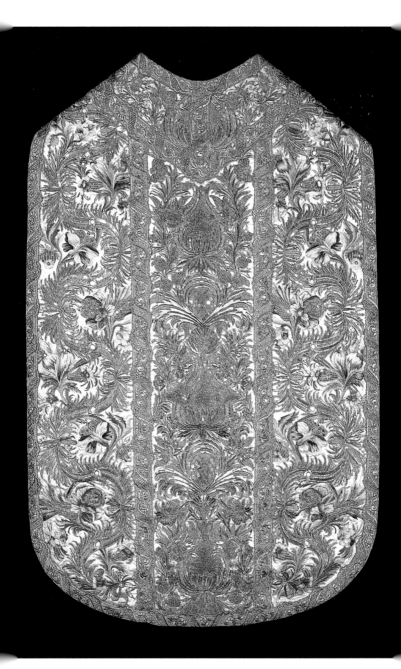

A chasuble from the 'Polling vestments', lavish embroidered pictures in gold
thread. The largest and most valuable group of vestments from this Upper Bavarian
monasteries was made in Munich in 1730/40 and was acquired for the Court
Chapel in 1803 after secularization.

The interior of the Reliquaries Chamber. In the foreground the 'Kindl Shrine', an ebony receptacle with engraved stones and cut glass panels to hold mummified children's bodies, Munich, 1611–26.

garded as the greatest treasure in the Residence. Some visitors might prefer to concentrate on the sumptuous settings and casings made to safeguard these precious relics. For those interested in the cultural and historical side of the collections, however, this is the very place for gaining more profound insights. New aspects of the grandiose ambitions entertained by Late Renaissance Wittelsbachs come to light and a better understanding of what moved Martin Luther to instigate the Reformation can be gained. One of the main abuses he was fighting was the exaggerated cult of relics observed in those tumultuous times. This is where religious controversies converge and the symbolic powers brought into play by the Residence as a flashpoint of European (religious) politics during the Counter-Reformation can be sensed. Although there is scarcely enough space to do justice to even seventy-six objects, the Residence Reliquaries Col-

lection is, besides the Geistliche Schatzkammer (Ecclisiastic Treasury) of the Viennese Hofburg, one of the most important exhibitions of European relics in a profane setting.

The Reliquary collection was founded in 1577, the year the Pope granted the right of collecting relics to the crown prince who would become Wilhelm v. He and his fellow Catholics were convinced that the cult of relics would be the best way of consolidating the Counter-Reformation in a place where Protestantism was especially critical. Moreover, the miraculous properties attributed to the relics collected seemed to offer a unique advantage in the conduct of *Realpolitik* whose significance can hardly be appreciated now. The Duke of Bavaria promoted several collections of relics, most of which have been lost. The Residence Museum is fortunate indeed in having fourteen prime exhibits from Wilhelm's era.

Duke Maximilian I considerably enlarged his father's collection and commissioned the building of the Rich Chapel (see p. 49) as a suitably sumptuous setting for the relics. Here the beleaguered monarch could gather strength in meditation and communion with martyred saints to fight his political battles. Gradually this room for private monarchical devotions became the most holy place in the Residence and, indirectly, in all Bavaria ruled by the original Wittelsbach line. Although only a few people were privileged to enter this chapel, early texts have a lot to say about the relics it contained for safe keeping. Later generations of rulers did little to add to the collection yet the nucleus has survived all crises through the commitment shown by its guardians.

Until the monarchy was abolished in 1918, a quaint congeries of relics and liturgical vessels was squeezed into the confined space afforded by the Rich Chapel. When the Residence Museum was founded, it was at first thought to be too risky to exhibit the collection there. It was displayed for a brief interlude in a vault-like room with more recent acquisitions from 1939, until the war made it imperative to shut down the exhibition. On reconstruction, major parts of the collection were given to the new Treasury and the Sacred Vestments Rooms. Nowadays only reliquaries with their contents intact are again displayed near the court chapels. Most of them are still owned by the House of Wittelsbach.

Monstrances

Relics are most effective when displayed in a ceremonial setting where the devout can see them. Precious vessels, known as monstrances, were made for this purpose. They enabled priests to use the relics and, at the same time, lent these inconspicuous scraps of cloth or splinters of bone mystical grandeur. The most elaborate and, at 115 cm, tallest, object of this type (21) here conceals the relics which were most venerated: a piece

Large reliquary in the shape of a monstrance of cast silver with pearls, precious stones and enamel (no. 21), probably made in the Augsburg workshop of Abraham Lotter after 1590. The transparent receptacles hold objects recalling the Passion.

of the blood-spattered column, at which Christ was scourged, soil from Calvary, thorns, a nail, tiny splinters of the True Cross, scraps of cloth and even a piece of the sponge which was soaked in vinegar, all purported to be authentic documents of the Crucifixion. The monstrance (unfortunately badly restored), of cast silver decorated with enamelled gold and set sumptuously with precious stones, is attributed to the Augsburg workshop of Abraham Lotter. Although it is dated to 1590, parts of it were probably not made until 1613. The Late Gothic monstrance shape has lived on here, with all its references to liturgial functions centring on the consecrated host kept in it, whose place is taken by the column fragment in the central receptacle. Around this, cylinders of glass have been arranged with the rest of the relics. Figurative scenes (executed in polychrome enamel on miniature statues cast in the round in gold) related to the relics displayed in the monstrance adorn its fantastic architecture, which reveals consummate artistry of workmanship. At the pier-like elements articulating the monstrance and on them as well personified monarchical virtues referring to Old Testament figures and the Apostles represent a comprehensive theological and iconographic programme. The monstrance was set up on its decorated ebony pedestal (17a) in the Rich Chapel so that it could be displayed by lowering the central silver relief of the altar.

Early Baroque forms are introduced by works (c. 1620) from the hand of the Munich master craftsman Bernhard Peter, who set the tops of the skulls of Saints Nicholas and Cyprian (58 and 59) in disc-shaped settings of precious stones. The exquisitely enamelled armorial bearings on the knop show that these reliquaries were donated by Duke Maximilian and his wife, Elisabeth of Lorraine. The Thirty Years' War put paid to the making of monstrances on such a lavish scale. Four mid-eighteenth-century monstrances (63–66) represent the modest vernacular style to which the cult of relics had descended by this time.

Reliquary in the form of a monstrance in four parts, silver-gilt, set with pearls and precious stones (no. 57). The top was made by Georg Jungmair of Augsburg in the 1620s; the fine pierced foot and cylinder containing relics of the Holy Blood date from the reign of Albrecht V.

Reliquary Shrines

Large relics, entire bodies of saints or a host of smaller relics which were meant to impress by their sheer number and could not be otherwise dealt with in a liturgical context, were consigned to reliquary shrines. Elaborate sacred appointments of this type, containing hundreds of relics each, were

Reliquary shrine of ivory with engraved glass panels and set with tear-drop coral (no. 53), made in 1624. Inside – according to the inventory – are the bones of Sts Servatius, Adrian, Boniface, Pancras and Christopher.

set up flanking the altar of the Rich Chapel, where they were destroyed by fire in 1944. Among the reliquary shrines that have survived, the Kindl Shrine (at the centre of the room) and a triad of glass reliquaries containing the relics of St Servatius (52–54) are particularly interesting.

The Massacre of the Innocents (Matt. 2, 13f) is regarded as the first martyrdom in the Christian sense. Duke Maximilian sought a more profound association to the event by acquiring one large and two smaller mummies purported to be those of children killed at Bethlehem. He had a small shrine made to house one of them and then, in 1626, a larger glass shrine was placed below it for the others. Made of ebony, decorated with the finest enamel on gold, precious stones and engraved stones, the reliquary is as fine in its way as the crystal shrine

owned by Duke Albrecht V in the Treasury and the case of the fine organ in the Rich Chapel. The rock-crystal windows through which the relics can be viewed are in part decorated with the donors' armorial bearings of Bavaria and Lorraine. The gruesome look inside shows the little mummified bodies bedded on and wrapped in exquisite embroidery.

The equally remarkable piece of miniature furniture enclosing the skull relic of St Servatius (52–54) was made (before 1624) by an unidentified Munich workshop. It belongs to a group of ivory-panelled luxury objects of which the most important is the coin shrine (1618–24) made by Christoph Angermair, now in the Bavarian National Museum. The delicate white of ivory was often combined with lapis lazuli to denote the Bavarian heraldic colours. White probably also stands

for the immaculate souls of the saints whose venerated relics are contained in the reliquaries here. Salmon-coloured tear-drop-shaped pieces of coral symbolize the blood of the martyrs. Of the many bones identified by scraps of parchment bearing names, the most important are those of Servatius. Said to have worked miracles in 350 AD in Tongeren, Belgium, Servatius is an 'Ice Saint' (feast day 13 May) who can make his influence felt on the unpredictable Munich weather.

Panel reliquary of ebony with enamelled gold mounts (no. 18), made in Munich in the 1580s. The plinth relief with representations of the Last Supper refers to the scraps of cloth contained in the reliquary, which were thought to have witnessed that event.

Reliquaries and Objects Decorated with Reliquaries

The other receptacles for holy relics exhibited here are of the more modest kind encountered in nearly all early Catholic churches and are dealt with here as a group. The most frequent type is the panel reliquary, which is like a devotional relief, followed by objects in the round which look like towers or

Skull reliquary (no. 48), covered in cloth embroidered with pearls, the work of Franz Joseph Anton Janssens (c. 1755), and a diadem of enamelled flowers. The inscription says that this was the head of St Elizabeth, the mother of John the Baptist.

Holy Water font shaped like an altar of gilt bronze inlaid with panels of lapis lazuli and mounted with relics (no. 67), made by Giovanni Giardini in Rome in 1709.

monstrances of the Gothic type. All types are impresssively represented in the Reliquaries Chamber.

A particularly elaborate panel (3), containing one large and three smaller scraps of cloth, is representative of the first group. The cloth is said to have been owned by the Virgin, who was especially venerated by the Wittels-

bachs. Its tracery of miniature architecture with arched gables and pilasters from the time of Duke Wilhelm V was modernized by the addition of a substucture like an altar table and side mounts by his successor. The additions are the work of Mathias Wallbaum of Augsburg. Among them, stylized serpents with enamelled scales represent a striking motif, executed with consummate technical mastery. They refer to the Woman of the Apocalypse in the Revelations of John the Divine and to the Virgin, who is depicted with one kick destroying evil on earth, symbolized by a reptile choking the orb of the world.

A reliquary (c. 1600) of the monstrance type is the work of Mathias Wallbaum, mentioned above. A pair of monstrances in which statuettes of the Virgin as Patrona Bavariae (26) and St Francis of Assisi (27) at the centre allude to the most important relics they contain are notable for the colour contrast between black and silver and the effective use of robustly carved wood set off by delicate mounts.

The special shape of the tower-like reliquaries were developed so that single, rather bulky pieces of bodies could be presented in a natural pose. The most impressive of these are four lantern-shaped metal receptacles (38–41) from the Augsburg workshop of Ulrich Ment (d. after 1623), which date from the third decade of the 17th century. According to the inscribed tablets and the little enamelled gold figures on them, they conceal the hands of St Denys the Areopagite, John the Baptist, St John Chrysostom and St Barbara, which are raised in the gesture of blessing. The armorial bearings on the substructure reveal that they were donated by the Duke and Duchess.

Some relics were displayed so that they could be touched by the devout using special gestures of veneration. Four complete skull relics attributed to the Popes Eleutherius (tenure 175–189) and Lucius (tenure 253–254; 19 and 20), John the Baptist and his mother, Elizabeth (47 and 48) are included in the collection. The skulls are encased in cloth, which, like the cushions on which they rest, is superbly embroidered, with only the foreheads exposed. The Papal skulls were exhibited with gilt tiaras in the mid-eighteenth

century. Munich craftsmen created filigree wreaths for the Holy Kinship, drawing on the entire repertoire which goldsmiths, jewellers and enamellers had at their disposal in 1620.

A last group of objects shows that the original religious idea behind the veneration of holy relics – keeping the memory of saints alive by creating appropriate casings for their mortal remains – was eclipsed by a new interest. Artists and their patrons set cult objects or even profane artefacts in daily use with relics to give them a religious character. This is a fundamental difference. The change can be interpreted positively as the suffusing of all areas of life with religious content, which was the declared intent of the Munich court in 1600. However, symptoms of an increasingly superficial attitude to religion were emerging concomitantly with Absolutism. As a countervailing force, the Enlightenment aimed at abolishing the ancient forms of government and, with their demise, intended to cut off the flowering branch of cultural history discussed here.

Five cross reliquaries illustrate this point. The earliest and most venerable of them (apart from the little Late Gothic crucifix which was put to a different use in the Baroque period, no. 73), is an ebony cross (c. 1590) without a crucified Christ, which is set off by five reliquary capsules (1). Although beautifully worked, the enamelled gold rosettes set with rubies were originally used as the buttons of robes of state.

Another piece of that type belongs to the most beautiful objects in the Reliquaries Chamber: the large pax tablet (42) with representations and minuscule relics (in the capital of the top of the handle) related to the birth and the Entombment of Jesus Christ. It was given the kiss of peace during Mass. Originally (c. 1570) it may have boasted a precious mirror, which, thus rededicated from the profane use of confirming vanity as a devotional object for Duke Wilhelm V may well have had symbolic meaning for him. The miniature paintings by the court painter Hans Werl after Hans von Aachen, who was celebrated in his day, make it possible to date the tablet to 1592. Duke Maximilian had a few last touches added in about 1620.

Leaving the Reliquaries Chamber, a magnificent Baroque wall decoration (67) uniting burnished gold with blue semiprecious stones cannot be missed. An allegorical relief with female personifications of peace and meekness indicates a general ethical content which makes the altar-shaped object's primary function as a holy water font appear irrelevant.

The Court Plate

The History of the Collection and how it is Exhibited

Elaborate formal banquets on a grand scale, accompanied by music and serving ceremonial, were among the earliest and most popular forms of court functions. Guests' rank was not last reflected by the plate and table decorations. Such questions of etiquette could be expressed in the use of gold, silver-gilt, silver and (for the lowest-ranking officials) pewter in descending order of importance. Solid silver tended to be the norm at the Munich court. Silver was not just used at the banquet table;

The 500-piece vermeil (silver-gilt) service owned by King Maximilian I. Made by Martin-Guillaume Biennais and Jean-Baptiste Odilot 1807–09 in Paris, it came to Munich in about 1816. The arrangement on the long table display case in the Hartschiersaal evokes royal banquets.

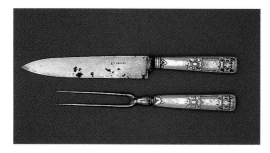

Cutlery with the coat of arms of Maximilian I as Prince Elector of Bavaria, steel with gold handles, c. 1600. Noticeably worn, these pieces were presumably used regularly by the statesman.

it accompanied the higher nobility throughout their lives as appropriate christening presents, sets of plate included in dowries and, finally, as coffin nails. The Silver Vaults were under the supervision of a Silver Chamberlain, who was responsible for keeping plate ready for use and caring for it. Plate was proverbially prized for its intrinsic value alone even more than other domestic treasures were and this led to disaster on numerous occasions.

Turreen pot à oille on matching plate, silver-gilt, acquired by Max Emmanuel, Prince Elector of Bavaria, in Brussels in about 1714. The armorial bearings show that he was then Stadholder of the Spanish Netherlands. The famous Spanish court soup 'olla podrida' was served in turreens of this type.

The history of all silver vaults is fraught with losses. This also holds for the Residence. In 1632 the Swedes looted it and, a decade later, when the court plate was being transferred to a safer place, it sank in the waters of the River Inn. Fortunately for modern scholarship, some pieces have been recovered from the shingle only very recently. The victors in the War of the Spanish Succession struck 40,000 guilders from the plate left behind by the Prince Elector Max Emmanuel, thus ignominiously destroying the superb seventeenth-century silver used by the Munich court at one go. Max-Emmanuel's grandson, Max III Joseph, philosophically took advantage of the next lost war of succession to replenish the decimated state treasury from the Silver Vault. From 1777 on it was refilled with pieces from the Palatinate Wittelsbachs. Fortunately, the turbulent Napoleonic War years before and after 1800 did not exact such a heavy toll in Bavarian court plate. From then on more silver was acquired than lost, starting with the silver confiscated during secularization. Since the Bavarian kings were by now enthusiastic givers of state banquets, a great deal more plate was needed. During World War II, the silver now displayed in the Museum was so well stored that most of it was saved. Possessing about 3,500 pieces, the Munich Silver Vaults share the honour of being among the world's richest along with the London, Stockholm and St Petersburg collections.

An inventory drawn up in about 1585 for Duke Wilhelm V indicates nearly 600 pieces, which, like the other treasures, were stored in the Neueste Silver Tower. Duke Maxmilian I provided spacious rooms in the Court Chapel Complex of his new Residence (the suite has been preserved in its original style; it now houses the vestment collections, see p. 106) before the Silver Tower was torn down in 1612. The function of the Vaults remained unchanged for three centuries until the

first Residence Museum renovated some ground-floor space at the western end of the Grotto Court for what was still a modest exhibition of silver. The present exhibition rooms were opened in 1974. Originally the Electresses' rooms of state, they were converted in the early nineteenth century to house the Bavarian Council of State, the king's cabinet. It is certainly regrettable that this fine monument to more recent Bavarian history should have been abandoned although its original appointments are for the most part preserved.

Detail of a silver wine cistern (used as a wine cooler) owned by the Prince Elector Max Emmanuel. Made in Paris by Claude Ballin the Younger in 1712.

A Brief Survey of the Exhibits

The silver collection starts in the Golden Hall (Room 71), which forms part of the Papal Chambers. A few silver-gilt pieces, which might just as well be

Silver warming-pan owned by Princess Charlotte Auguste, a daughter of King Maximilian I, made c. 1810. Once fitted with a long wooden handle and filled with live coals, the vessel was used to warm the royal bed.

Powder jar from the Strasbourg Silver, made ca 1786 by Johann Jakob Kirstein on the birth of the crown prince, later King Ludwig I. The Wittelsbachs of the Palatinate line brought this and other fine pieces to Munich after 1777.

kept in the Treasury, convey some idea of the lost Late Renaissance plate.

The First Silver Chamber (Room 100) is devoted to late eighteenth-century silver. A considerable number of chargers and candelabra, all rather similar in style, a feature which carries over to the other display rooms, conveying a general impression of what the royal silver was like but tending to divert one's attention from the really important pieces and what they might have to tell us about history. Take a look at the very worn-looking cutlery in the table display case to the left of the entrance. Since they sport the coat of arms of Duke Maximilian I (*c.* 1600), these are the earliest pieces of their kind in the collection. Does this touchingly used-looking cutlery bring the daily life of Bavaria's great Prince Elector closer to us? Some of the uniformly shaped beakers which stand in a row on the middle shelf of the large display case are marked with the date 1667. They are all that remains of the everyday silver used in the reign of the Prince Elector Ferdinand Maria. The Prince Elector Max Emmanuel brought the magnificent 'wine cistern' (a type of cooler in which wine bottles were transported) on the lower part of the wall as you enter, a work by the Paris silversmith Claude II Ballin, back with him from exile in France in 1715. With a few other pieces it represents the elegant banqueting culture that reigned in Late Baroque Munich. Simpler pieces from this period reveal an astonishing continuity of form and this consoles us for the great losses of 'everyday service'. Finally, take note of four oval sideboard dishes in the middle of the wall as you enter the room. Sporting a combination of the Electoral coat of arms, various other armorial bearings, and the double-headed imperial eagle, they were ordered by the Prince Elector Karl Albrecht in 1740 to mark his appointment as Viceregent, that is, as one of the interim rulers after the death of the Emperor Charles VI. The

Table decoration shaped like a wine crater with openwork decoration. Made by the Munich silversmith Anton Weishaupt in 1830 as part of a large silver service on the French model.

appointment of a Wittelsbach to this position presaged the territorial wars that would follow the extinction of the male branch of the Habsburg line.

The Second Silver Chamber (Room 101) has been set aside for the plate brought from the Palatinate. The most impressively sumptuous pieces were made by Strasbourg silversmiths for the elder brother of the prince who would become King Max I. In the two other rooms – the Third Silver Chamber and the Hartschiersaal, which is also used to house the silver collections – silver made for the young kindom of Bavaria is displayed, recognisable by the royal armorial bearings on it. There are two extraordinarily grand sets (later additions to them will be passed over here). First, there are pieces from a silver service with lavish moulded decoration which the Augsburg firm of Joseph Anton Seethaler delivered to the court in the first decade of the

nineteenth century. Ten years later an even more ornate service came on the market: consisting of more than 500 pieces of vermeil or silver-gilt, it was owned by Jérôme Bonaparte before he was deposed as King of Westphalia. Made by the French silversmith Martin-Guillaume Biennais, who was already known in Munich as the maker of the Bavarian crown insignia, it was sold to the Munich court through the agency of the firm of Seethaler. This service and its arrangement in a large showcase demonstrates most clearly how the royal banquet table looked when it was set and how the treasures in the Silver Chambers were used.

Display rooms of the East Asian Collection in the rear rooms of the Electoral apartments. Behind a group of Japanese porcelain dishes and vases hangs one of the 'Polonaise Rugs', once part of the dowry of a Polish princess and woven in Kashan, Persia, in the seventeenth century.

The East Asian Collection

The History of the Munich Collection

In the late thirteenth century Marco Polo introduced a mysterious white pottery to Europe which he called 'porcellana' after the shell of the cowrie, a marine mollusc. So highly sophisticated was Chinese culture by Polo's time that Chinese craftsmen had discovered the process for making it five hundred years before his travels. Japanese porcelain is considerably later; porcelain-making did not develop in Japan until raw materials were available in sufficient quantities from the sixteenth century. The porcelain Japan exported to the west was named after the trading port of Imari. It was quite difficult to acquire East Asian porcelain in Europe at first. Pieces of Chinese porcelain were such highly prized items in Late Gothic Kunstkammer

that mounts of precious metals were made for many of them. Contacts with the Jesuit mission in the Far East enabled the Dukes of Bavaria to acquire their first pieces of 'white gold'. An inventory drawn up in 1598 has entries for 170 pieces, most of which were lost in the Thirty Years' War.

The Munich porcelain collection owes its greatest debt to the Prince Elector Max Emmanuel. As Stadholder of the Spanish Netherlands in Brussels, he took advantage of any opportunities offered to buy porcelain sold by Dutch East India traders, who had been bringing it back as ballast, so cheap was it, in the spice ships since the early seventeenth century. The early eighteenth-century mania for chinoiserie, which enriched architecture, furnishings and textiles, was another positive element of the china trade. In 1693/94 a room was allocated to the display of porcelain in the Munich Residence for the first time. Designated the Dutch Cabinet, it reveals the provenance of its costly exhibits. The fire of 1729 destroyed it. François Cuvilliés used pieces of Far Eastern porcelain to decorate the walls of the Rich Rooms which followed it. Over a hundred consoles sport small vases between the large glass surfaces of the Mirror Cabinet (see p. 76) which translate them into multiple reflections. Vessels and chargers were displayed on furniture or chimney-pieces. Together with porcelain figures combined with clock cases or candelabra they still adorn the formal rooms of the Residence.

Imported ware was no longer so coveted after Europeans had discovered the secret of making porcelain. An exhibition mounted by the Bavarian National Museum in 1909, however, revived interest in Far Eastern porcelain. Not until 1937 was a special display of it, albeit in rather cramped quarters, set up in the Residence. The suite in which it was housed was destroyed in 1944 and reconstruction eventually led to the creation of a neutral environment where these treasures, which had all been stored safely during the war, have been displayed since 1966.

Since the objects exhibited are all of Asian origin, the Entrance Hall (Room 15) is largely devoted to a display of a series of seventeenth-century Persian carpets. The so-called Polish rugs may have formed part of the dowry of a Polish-born Palatinate electress and, as such, came in the possession of the Wittelsbachs. In this respect there are, however, still a number of questions that remain unanswered. The most valuable piece is now to be found in the last room of the Treasury (see p. 105).

The Most Important Period Styles in East Asian Porcelain

Dating Chinese porcelain is difficult. Reign marks in seal characters are usually decipherable but fakes and the use of earlier period marks on later pieces frequently occur. To help you find your

Chinese blue-and-white ware dating from c. 1600. The elaborate metal mount shows that this simple bowl was among the items in the Kunstkammer of Duke Wilhelm V, which means that it is one of the earliest pieces of East Asian porcelain in the Residence collections.

way about the exhibition, the reign periods represented by porcelain in the Residence collection are listed in the following table:

Ming Reign Periods:
Xuande   1426–35
Chenghua   1465–87
Zhengde   1506–21
Jiajing   1522–66
Wanli   1573–1619

Qing or Manchu Reign Periods:
Kangxi   1662–1722
Yongzheng   1723–35
Qianlong   1736–95

Stylistic features are, therefore, the definitive criterion for identification. Among the earliest pieces, blue-and-white ware predominates. Its decoration is underglaze blue. During the early seventeenth century it became fashionable to add iron-red, copper-green and occasionally even gold and subject such pieces to a second firing. Because this tricolour ware is similar in some respects to Japanese wares made at the same time, it is called 'Chinese Imari'. The prolific period shortly before and after 1700 saw additions to the palette, with greens predominating: '*famille-verte*', a familiar sight in

Chinese porcelain ginger jar, Kangxi period (1662–1722). Plum branches alive with birds and insects are set off by vibrant greens, indicating that this is a piece of famille verte.

European and American collections; or pinks, a style known as '*famille-rose*'. The latter style was especially popular in Holland. However, monochrome glazes, notably '*celadon*' ware in light green with a greyish or blueish cast, marking a reversion to earlier wares,

Porcelain charger, famille rose with a scene from a romance: a lady is giving a mounted knight a drink. China, mid-eighteenth century. The name famille rose comes from the broken reds predominating in late pieces such as this.

were also greatly appreciated. Ware from Jingdezhen, where earlier Ming was reproduced on a large scale, and monochrome white to cream-glazed Dehua wares, the latter represented by vessels with relief decoration and figures, are also present in the Residence collection.

Japanese porcelain was usually fired three times. 'Arita Imari' from Japan is notable for minutely detailed decoration. Further, the cobalt blue of the Japanese ware tends to be more vibrant than on Chinese Imari although it is often difficult to distinguish the two. Japanese porcelain painting on imported ware proved easy to reproduce in Europe.

Cup and cover with saucer, dated by French silver mount to before 1710. The colours are typical of Chinese Imari: deep underglaze blue, iron-red and gold.

A Brief Survey of the Exhibition

The first room of the East Asian collection (Room 15) is stocked with classic *famille-verte* and *famille-rose*. A particularly fine piece is a bowl decorated

Elephant, white Japanese porcelain converted in Paris (c. 1720) into the support for a table or mantel clock.

with stylized floral scrollwork, which is exhibited with classic blue-and-white ware. An unpretentious piece, it dates from the Wanli period and was mounted in silver in about 1600 as rare collector's items so often were in South Germany. This may, therefore be one of the few pieces to have survived from the ducal Kunstkammer.

The second room of the East Asian collection (Room 16) is devoted to figures, such as a group of mythical beasts with the attributes of Buddhist mythology. Known as 'Fo dogs', they were made in the '*email-sur-biscuit*' technique: the turquoise and aubergine glaze was applied on the biscuit and the piece was fired a second time. The Kangxi group was clustered in mid-eighteenth-century France about a clock case and furnished with a European-looking substructure. A group of eighteenth -century cache-pots was

given similar treatment. Arriving in Europe as garden stools with an 'archaic' celadon glaze, they were separated in a Paris workshop and embellished with gilded bronze mounts.

An early eighteenth-century Paris inkstand is exhibited in the Third East Asian Room (Room 17). It is a combination of various Dehua pieces in the popular monochrome '*blanc-de-Chine*' glaze. Decorated with moulded flowers, the three vessels were used as a quill-holder, inkpot and pounce-pot for sand to blot ink. The garniture of vases on the far side of the passage is a rare example of the lustrous 'mirror-black' monochrome glaze produced in China in 1700 and decorated with fine gold designs.

The room which was once St Cecilia's Chapel (Room 18), near where Max Emmanuel's Dutch Cabinet is thought to have been, boasts an exhibit

Vase, square in section, with typical 'Kakiemon painting'. Light, forceful, sparsely distributed figures on a milky white ground are all features typical of the work of the famous early seventeenth-century painter of that name. Japanese Kakiemon came from Arita in the western province of Hizen.

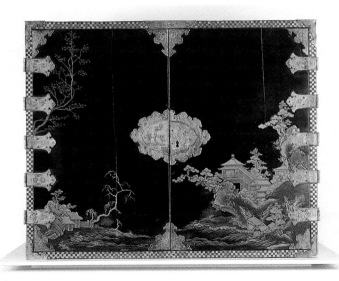

Japanese lacquer cabinet, early 18th-century. A landscape in sprinkled gold technique is picked out on the glossy black 'urushi' ground.

of artefacts representing the assimilation of East Asian influence. Dishes which were originally white were painted, presumably in the Netherlands. In this case they were decorated with the combined armorial bearings signifying a royal marriage, which date them to about 1710. This large set of dishes came to Munich from the Palatinate.

The fifth room (Room 19) invites visitors to compare Chinese and Japanese porcelain. Motifs from Chinese porcelain are juxtaposed – e.g. blue-red-and-gold Japanese and Chinese Imari – with their Japanese counterparts. A remarkable piece decorated with casually composed vitrified painting is from the hand of Sakaida Kakiemon (1595–1666), who translated forms from traditional prints to the new medium of porcelain and exerted a profound stylistic influence on Europe.

The adjacent sixth room (Room 20) affords further opportunities for comparing sumptuous Japanese and Chinese furnishings. A Japanese lacquer cabinet and a Chinese wall screen represent the second important Far Eastern medium to have been coveted by 17th and 18th-century Europe: lacquer. Exacting consummate skill of its practitioners, lacquer painting after East Asian models was a craft much prized in Europe. Lacquer furniture frames and wall panelling were only two of the applications. The Rich Rooms in the Residence possess some fine examples (see p. 77). The East Asian Collection finishes with textiles of Asian provenance and two imposing *famille-rose* covered vases (Room 21).

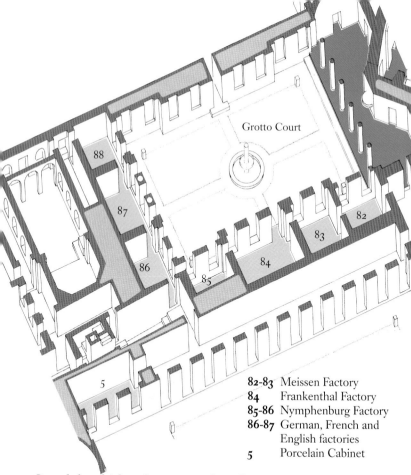

Grotto Court

82-83 Meissen Factory
84 Frankenthal Factory
85-86 Nymphenburg Factory
86-87 German, French and
English factories
5 Porcelain Cabinet

General plan of eighteenth-century porcelain collection

Below: Room 84 with Frankenthal porcelain

Eighteenth-century Porcelain

From the sixteenth century European craftsman had been trying to reproduce porcelain of a quality comparable with East Asian imports. Not until the early 18th century was a Dresden scientist, Ehrenfried Walter von Tzschirnhaus (1651–1708) able to make high-fired red stoneware and, in 1708, hard-paste biscuit porcelain. His assistant, Johann Friedrich Böttger, perfected the process and from 1710 headed the first European porcelain factory in Meissen which still exists today. The recipe for making porcelain could not be kept secret for long. By 1717 makers of porcelain at Meissen helped a Viennese entrepreneur to open a second European porcelain factory in his native city. Not long afterwards, employee disloyalty on similar lines took the secret to Venice. Early success in Vienna encouraged the Munich court of the Prince Elector Karl Albrecht to experiment with porcelain-making but a swindle put an end to these early efforts. Porcelain was not successfully made in Munich until 1754 after the War of the Austrian Succession had ended. From 1761 to the present day porcelain has been made at Nymphenburg. Other important porcelain factories were Frankenthal (1755–1799), financed by the Palatine court, and the Sèvres Factory, which was granted a state monopoly by the French king in 1756.

The Prince Elector Max Emmanuel was the first Wittelsbach to acquire Meissen porcelain. After his grandson, Max III Joseph, married a Saxon princess in 1747, the Munich court was won over to the prevailing enthusiasm for this luxurious china. A great deal of porcelain was bought before Munich finally had a porcelain factory of its own. Samples submitted for royal approval formed the basis of a collection which soon began to fill another court treasure chamber. After the Frankenthal Factory closed down, important pieces from it went to Munich, as they had in 1777, when Karl Theodor, the Elector Palatine, inherited the Bavarian crown. Presents, legacies and finally secularization continued to enlarge the collection. When King Ludwig II ascended the throne, a great deal of porcelain was ordered for him. Not much more of this has remained in the Residence than of the earlier pieces, many of the earliest of which were transferred to the Bavarian National Museum in the late nineteenth century. What is even more unfortunate is that porcelain was used at court every day and quite a lot was broken before it

A candelabrum with a stag mounted in gilt bronze. This early Meissen piece (c. 1725) shows East Asian influence.

could be declared museum property. By 1911 the most important groups of porcelain figures were suitably exhibited in François Cuvilliés' treasure vaults (see illus. p. 97), which were left unoccupied at the turn of the century when a new treasure chamber (now the Old Treasury) was built. It still houses a stylishly mounted exhibition representing a cross-section of European porcelain to match the history of the interiors.

Johann Joachim Kändler, porcelain group 'Fox accompanying a lady on the harpsichord', Meissen Factory after 1743. This witty piece may be a covert allusion to the liaison between the Viennese Court bandmaster, Johann Joseph Fux (meaning fox), and the celebrated singer Faustina Bordoni.

The earlier Residence Museum grouped the entire porcelain collection in the suite of rooms where it is still exhibited. Since only the four southern rooms were available, the china, piled up in cupboards, was not set off well enough. Reconstruction after the war afforded a good opportunity of reorganising the display of those pieces which had survived transferral to storage. Since 1958 they have been exhibited for the most part according to factory. Ambitiously realised, the exhibition space represents a highlight of conservative 1950s museum design.

The Meissen Factory

The best place to start your tour of the First and Second Porcelain Chambers (Rooms 82 and 83) is with the historic beginnings of native European porcelain: Meissen. Meissen modellers and porcelain-painters at first stuck quite closely to Asian models. European motifs after contemporary engravings were painted on Meissen pieces by Augsburg painters, for instance on a breakfast service (*c.* 1730). The earliest European porcelain figures represent genre scenes and animals, both originating in chinoiserie.

Johann-Gregor Höroldt (1696–1775) was the founder of the great school of Meissen porcelain-painting. A tea service in the collection reveals his signature although the general level of craftsmanship was so high that collaboration on such sets can be assumed. Höroldt's major technical innovation was a rich palette of basic colours, which widened the Meissen scope to include the light yellow, peach-bloom and celebrated sea-green represented in the Residence collection.

Flamboyantly overshadowing Höroldt, Johann Joachim Kändler (1706–1775) made porcelain figures a star attraction of the Meissen repertoire and they have remained coveted collector's items to this day. Kändler is given to genre scenes, which reflect court life in pastoral guise. Numerous important figures of saints, exemplified by an Immaculata (1730s), evoke the religious fervour of their time. Mould-ed elements now began to become increasingly important as decoration on fine porcelain tableware. A breakfast service (*c.* 1740), charmingly decorated with painted insects and flowers in relief, marks the beginning of a development which led to sumptuous table decorations covered with a profusion of delicate white sprigged flowers. This stylistic trend culminated in vessels made as realistic imitations of fruits and vegetables. Kändler in his turn was supplanted in 1765 by a Frenchman, Michel-Victor Acier, whose group of

Johann Joachim Kändler or possibly Michel-Victor Acier: 'The Judgement of Paris', Meissen Factory, c. 1760. Bisque table decoration.

Johann Wilhelm Lanz, table decoration 'Venus at her toilet', Frankenthal, c. 1760. This three-figure piece in its lavish rocaille arbour was the largest porcelain sculpture made by the Palatinate factory.

In the manner of Johann-Gregor Höroldt, vase with chinoiserie scene in a reserve on a yellow ground, Meissen Factory c. 1730.

figures representing the Judgement of Paris (*c.* 1760) stands at the centre of the second porcelain room. In the Rococo period Meissen porcelain sculpture attained a second flowering, represented here by this ten-piece group. Acier's later work in the early Neo-Classical style goes beyond the bounds of the eighteenth-century collection.

The Frankenthal Factory

The third porcelain chamber (Room 84) is devoted to the Palatinate porcelain factory which was founded by the Strasbourg faïence-maker Paul Hanong in Frankenthal. Karl Theodor, then the Elector Palatine, was enlightened enough to see the advantages of backing this new growth industry which in 1762 was taken over by the state. With a repertoire of over 800 models, Frankenthal was more than a match for Meissen in the field of porcelain sculpture. The turmoil of the French Revolution ended production at Frankenthal; its leading craftsmen moved to Bavaria in 1799, where they made a welcome addition to the Nymphenburg Factory staff. The treasure trove of 283 chests of porcelain which they brought with them founded the world's largest and most valuable collection of Frankenthal hard-paste porcelain. Its finest pieces are displayed in the Residence.

The first Frankenthal modeller was Johann Wilhelm Lanz. His masterpiece, a delicately tinted *Venus at her toilet* set suggestively in C-scroll rocaille licking up like the slap and tickle of a wave is a tour de force of superb craftsmanship. From 1758 Lanz collaborated with an assistant modeller, Johann Friedrich Lück, who had trained under Kändler. The first star modeller at Frankenthal was, however, Konrad Link (1732–93), who had trained in Vienna and Berlin as a sculptor. Before returning to monumental sculpture in 1766, he left a legacy of lyrical creations like the *Atalante and Meleager* and a Four Seasons cycle in Frankenthal which reveal him as the equal of Kändler and the Nymphenburg master modeller Bustelli.

In Frankenthal porcelain-painting took second place – not in quality – to figure modelling. The Residence possesses an important thrity-two-piece service (1771) decorated with birds. A garniture of vases decorated in red with theatre scenes after Watteau, which was made in the early years at Frankenthal, is particularly fine.

Cooler from the 'Large Birds Service', Frankenthal Factory, c. 1771. Working under the masters Osterspey and Winterstein, porcelain painters have come up with a superb pheasant. This service well bears comparison with the Sèvres Bird Service in the collection.

Turreen from the Beaded Service, Nymphenburg Factory 1792–95. Dominkus Auliczek of Bohemia designed this elegant 350-piece service. Already Neo-Classical in form, all pieces are dodecahedral in section.

Nymphenburg Porcelain

The Bavarian porcelain factory is superbly represented in the large Bäuml Collection as well as the Bavarian National Museum. However, for a survey of European porcelain at its zenith, the Residence Museum is a must, especially the fourth and fifth rooms of this Porcelain Collection (Rooms 85 and 86). Nymphenburg porcelain looks back on a varied and turbulent history.

May it suffice to observe here that it was founded by the entrepreneur Franz Ignaz Niedermaier. Technical aid from the Viennese Factory enabled it by 1754 to reach the standards of craftsmanship it needed to attract court patronage. The Prince Elector Max III took it under his wing, placing Sigmund, Count Haimhausen, in charge and promoting it so successfully that it moved in 1761 to its present premises next to the royal summer residence, where it continues flourish to this day.

The flowering of the Nymphenburg Factory coincided with the most important creations of the most famous Nymphenburg modeller, Franz Anton Bustelli (active in Munich from 1754

Franz Anton Bustelli, 'Apple-Woman', Nymphenburg Factory c. 1755. A little genre figure typical of work by the most talented and even today most popular modeller at the Munich workshop.

until his death in 1763), who was a virtuoso of his craft. His early work is represented in the Residence by scenes of court masquerades and *fêtes galantes* of a liveliness hitherto unattained in the genre. His masterpiece is a group of 16 'Commedia dell'arte' characters, eight of which are shown in the Residence. Unpainted, they are particularly effective as miniature sculpture.

In the fourth porcelain room early Munich porcelain is shown in a setting reminiscent of the interior decoration which once reigned supreme here. A parquetry floor, a fireplace surrounded in marble, a portrait of Max III Joseph, an avid collector of porcelain, and a matching display case recall the ' Yellow Suite' of private apartments occupied by the Prince Elector Karl Albrecht. Designed by François Cuvilliés the Elder, they were, unfortunately, completely redesigned in the nineteenth century.

The exhibition room which follows is devoted to the largest everyday service, comprising about 350 pieces decorated with landscape motifs, made in Nymphenburg in the late eighteenth century. Based on the dodecahedron and decorated in Bavarian blue and white, it sports beaded borders, which gave it its name. In the midst of all these witnesses to elegant court banqueting, is a series of figures of the Olympian gods, skillfully modelled by Dominikus Auliczek (1704–73), a Bohemian craftsman who shaped the course of events in porcelain sculpture for decades at the Nymphenburg Factory. Had he not been the successor of the brilliant Bustelli, he would enjoy the reputation he so richly deserves.

Sèvres and other European Porcelain Factories

The creatively shaped and coloured pieces made by the artists in porcelain most closely linked with the Wittelsbachs are contrasted in the last two

Charger from the Birds Service, Sèvres, 1759.

rooms (Rooms 87 and 88) with comparable pieces from other German and European centres. Individual pieces from the Ludwigsburg Factory in Baden-Württemberg, Höchst belonging to the Electoral court of Mainz and the Imperial Viennese Porcelain Factory round off the display in the last rooms.

Porcelain which was sent to Munich to consolidate Wittelsbach relations with Versailles is appropriately represented on a grand scale. The sixth room of the Porcelain Cabinet boasts a vast Sèvres service, decorated with a superbly painted cycle of birds, which was sent by Louis XV to the court of the Elector Palatine in 1760 as a diplomatic present. Then there is an inkstand with globes, exemplifying the mastery of form and delicacy of painting which French court art could command in its last flowering. Unfortunately, a rumour that this cabinet piece, owned by Madame de Pompadour, who did a lot to promote the Sèvres Factory, was a gift from the unhappy Marie-Antoinette, cannot be verified.

The 19th-century porcelain collection in the King's Building. In the foreground the purple 'Onyx Service', commissioned by King Ludwig I. By 1848 it comprised 717 pieces.

A putto writing the name of Karl Theodor, Prince Elector of Bavaria. Porcelain biscuit, probably made by Diehl & Guerhard, Paris c. 1795.

Nineteenth-century Porcelain

The History of the Collection

The later porcelain in the Residence Museum was, like the eighteenth-century services, used and stored with the plate until the monarchy was abolished. The earlier Residence Museum did not separate the two because stylistic boundaries tended to become blurred around 1800. Reconstruction planning for the Residence from the mid-1960s was influenced by the increasing appreciation of art which set in during the 19th century, making the decorative and applied arts appear in Germany in a new light. Exhibition space was created by 1974 for the collection of 19th-century porcelain when the eastern tract of the main floor of the King's Building was rebuilt to house the battle paintings (see p. 89). The back rooms in the apartments of King Ludwig I, former dining rooms, which had partly been given up for workshops, were ideal for the purpose. Decorated like the Battle Halls with reticent ashlar painting, these low-ceilinged rooms still reveal links with their former Neo-Classical splendour.

nineteenth century, with its meticulously executed and complex motifs as cycles deserving of careful study.

French Factories

Bavaria was traditionally close to France, culminating in the alliance with Napoleon, the elevation of the Prince Elector Max IV Joseph to King of Bavaria (from 1 January 1806 as Maximilian I) and the marriage between the

Pierced-work fruit basket with floral border on a gold ground. From the large Sèvres Flower Service made in 1808 and given by Napoleon to the Bavarian king.

The Munich porcelain collection is notable for presenting large services as if the pieces were set out for us (just think of the beaded service and the enormous eighteenth-century services). This feature of the exhibitions becomes especially noticeable in the nineteenth-century section. Being confronted with hundreds of matching pieces comprising a large service might at first seem overwhelming. However, it is best to view the porcelain painting, which grew in importance during the

Emperor's stepson and the Bavarian princess Auguste Amalie. Napoleon considered Max I even more important to cultivate as an ally against Austria than some of his more powerful cohorts because Max I represented the old royal families which the Corsican upstart hoped to win over as a first step to founding a dynasty of his own. The alliance was concluded with the exchange of costly presents. The Munich court also placed extensive orders with Paris ateliers. Both the Treasury and the Porcelain Cabinet profited from this diplomatic activity and the porcelain services have remained intact. The exhibition of porcelain from French factories (Room 14d) centres on a '*service encyclopédique*' from what was now known as the Imperial Sèvres Factory, presented by Napoleon in 1810. It comprises seventy-seven plates decorated with campaign and genre scenes in grisaille by Jacques-François Joseph Swebach, called Fontaine. The lavishly gilt flower service which Queen Karoline ordered from Sèvres was not a diplomatic present. A dessert service from the Paris firm of Stone-

Nymphenburg Porcelain

Bavarian porcelain is exhibited in the Nymphenburg Factory rooms (14e and 14f). Nymphenburg's fortunes were shaped during the first two decades of the 19th century by Johann Peter Melchior (1747–1825), who had moved to Munich from the Frankenthal Factory. During his tenure a large-scale project was launched which aimed at copying on porcelain the finest paintings in the royal galleries. Long before colour photography had been invented, painting on porcelain was the most durable way of preserving colour quality for

Peter Paul Rubens, Portrait of Hélène Fourment. King Ludwig I had this and other paintings in the Alte Pinakothek copied on porcelain so that their true colours might be handed down to posterity.

Coquerel and Legros d'Anisy comprises over 200 pieces decorated with scenes from Roman history according to Livy and European landscapes.

Individual pieces from smaller French factories, which had proved increasingly skilful at bypassing the state monopoly since the 1770s, are exhibited in the cabinet abutting to the east. Typical of the figures made in 1800, a putto in white biscuit made by Diehl et Guerhard in Paris pays tribute to Karl Theodor as Prince Elector of Bavaria.

posterity. Crown Prince Ludwig commissioned a series of plates from 1810; twenty-one of these are exhibited here. They were painted by Anton Auer, Louis-Socrate Fouquet and Christian Adler. From 1827 such paintings were no longer executed on pieces which formed part of services. Special large-scale ceramic plaques were invented for this purpose which reproduced the original proportions of the paintings. Although some were lost in the war, the most important of these replicas are exhibited in Room 14f. Appointing

Two plates and a fruit basket from the Onyx Service, Nymphenburg Factory, 1834–1848.

the distinguished architect Friedrich Gärtner as head designer at the Nymphenburg Factory Ludwig I signalized his personal commitment to porcelain manufacture as part of an economic growth programme promoting cultural development. The largest order placed was for the 717-piece Onyx Service (from 1834). Its name derives from the splendid Pompeiian red ground of the plates, dishes and other vessels designed to recall Greco-Roman antiquity. The picture reserves on the main pieces contain paintings of ancient sculpture, documenting what was by now exhibited in the Glyptothek. From 1842 more series of painted plates were ordered which, once again in brilliant colour, reproduced Bavarian landscapes after Quaglio, scenes from the *Nibelungenlied* and Bavarian dress with its local variants.

Porcelain from the Royal Prussian Porcelain Manufactory

The Porcelain Cabinet exhibitions close with the Royal Berlin Factory (Room 14g). It became important at the Munich Court in 1842, when the Crown Prince, Maximilian (II), married Marie of Prussia. This alliance would have been impossible in the 18th century because Prussia was Protestant and Bavaria Catholic but Bavaria had since become far more tolerant in religious matters. After all, it had had to integrate a large Protestant Franconian population after 1806. After initial difficulties as a private firm, the Prussian Porcelain Factory was granted a royal patent in 1763 as the Königlich-Preussische Porzellanmanufaktur (KPM) and underwent an upturn. It came into its own in the early 19th century through collaboration with such famous names as the sculptor Gottfried Schadow and the architects Hans Christian Genelli and even Karl Friedrich Schinkel. The large service sent by the Hohenzollerns as a wedding present to Maximilian and Marie of Prussia shows the KPM at its best. Blue and gold decoration with floral borders stands out strikingly against a white background. Table decorations, including Neo-Classical groups of figures in biscuit are a distinctive feature. The exhibition comes to a finale surprising in such a stronghold of Bavarian tradition with four magnificent blue-and-gold *Prunkvasen* sporting vedute of Berlin and dating from about 1830.

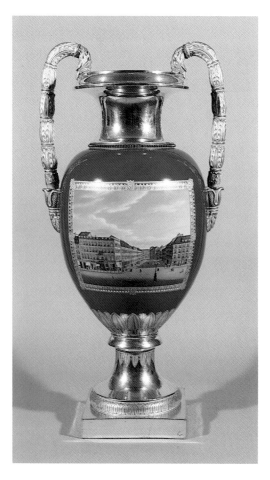

Allied by marriage since 1842, the Wittelsbachs and the Hohenzollerns exchanged costly presents such as this Prunkvase with a view of Breite Strasse in Berlin, made there ca. 1840.

SELECTED BIBLIOGRAPHY

History of the Residence

Bayerische Verwaltung der staatlichen Schlösser, Gärten und Seen, *Residenz München*, Munich 1996

Bayern, Adalbert Prinz von, *Als die Residenz noch Residenz war* (3rd ed.), Munich 1982

Haeutle, Christian. *Geschichte der Residenz in München von ihren frühesten Zeiten herab bis zum Jahre 1777*, Leipzig 1883

Klingensmith, Samuel John, *The Utility of Splendor, Ceremony, Social Life, and Architecture at the Court of Bavaria, 1600–1800*, Chicago/London 1993

Meitinger, Otto. 'Die baugeschichtliche Entwicklung der Neuveste'. In *Oberbayerisches Archiv*, Vol. 92, Munich 1970

Pistorini, Baldassare. 'Descrittione compendiosa del palagio sede de' Serenissimi di Baviera', Munich 1644 (manuscript, Bayerische Staatsbibliothek)

Walz, Tino, Otto Meitinger and Toni Beil, *Die Residenz zu München, Entstehung – Zerstörung – Wiederaufbau*, Munich 1987

Restored Rooms and Collections

Bauer, Hermann and Bernhard Rupprecht (eds.), with Anna Bauer-Wild and Brigitte Volk-Knüttel. 'Corpus der barocken Deckenmalerei in Deutschland', Vol. 3/II, Munich 1989

Bayerische Verwaltung der staatlichen Schlösser, Gärten und Seen. *Schatzkammer der Residenz München*, Munich 1992

Brunner, Herbert and Albrecht Miller (eds.). *Die Kunstschätze der Münchner Residenz*, Munich 1977

Heym, Sabine. *Das Alte Residenztheater/Cuvilliéstheater in München*, Munich 1995

Hojer, Gerhard. 'Die Prunkappartements Ludwigs I. im Königsbau der Münchner Residenz', *Architektur und Dekoration*, Munich 1992

Hojer, Gerhard and Hans Ottomeyer (eds.), compiled by Brigitte Langer, Alexander Herzog v. Württemberg et al. *Die Möbel der Residenz München*, Vols. I-III, Munich, London, New York 1995, 1996, 1997

Seelig Lorenz. *Kirchliche Schätze aus bayerischen Schlössern* (exhib. cat.), Munich 1984

Volk-Knüttel, Brigitte. *Wandteppiche für den Münchner Hof nach Entwürfen von Peter Candid*, Munich 1976

Weski, Ellen and Heike Frosien-Leinz (et al.). *Das Antiquarium der Münchner Residenz, Katalog der Skulpturen*, 2 vols., Munich 1987

Artists, Architects and Their Patrons

Braunfels, Wolfgang. *François Cuvilliés. Der Baumeister der galanten Architektur des Rokoko*, Munich 1986

Buttlar, Adrian von. *Leo von Klenze: Leben – Werk – Vision*, Munich 1999

Kraus, Andreas. *Maximilian I. Bayerns Großer Kurfürst*, Graz 1990

Nerdinger, Winfried (ed.). *Leo von Klenze, Architekt zwischen Kunst und Hof 1784–1864*, Munich 2000

Rall, Hans and Marga. *Die Wittelsbacher in Lebensbildern*, Graz 1986

Index of Names and Places

Italics refer to pages with illustrations

Photographic credits

The photographs reproduced here are from the Bayerischen Verwaltung der staatlichen Schlösser, Gärten und Seen and by the following photographers and archivists:

Bayerische Staatsbibliothek, Munich 13

Bayerische Staatsgemäldesammlungen, Munich 23

Bayerisches Nationalmuseum, Munich 20

Bunz, Achim, Munich (for the Bayerische Schlösserverwaltung) front cover, 10, 29, 30, 33, 34, 36, 37, 39 bottom, 40, 41 top, 44 top and bottom, 46/47, 58, 68, 70, 80, 81, 86, 87, 91, 94, 106, 110, 117, 122, 124 bottom, 127, 132 bottom, 136 top

Herzog-August-Bibliothek Wolfenbüttel 39 top

Münchner Stadtmuseum 14

Münchner Stadtmuseum, Franz Hanfstaengl Estate 22 bottom

Pulfer, Wolfgang, Munich 118 top

Seyerlein, Johannes, Munich 82, 83